Everyman's Poetry

*Everyman, I will go with thee,
and be thy guide*

John Clare

Selected and edited by R. K. R. THORNTON

University of Birmingham

EVERYMAN

J. M. Dent · London

Introduction and other critical apparatus
© J. M. Dent 1997

Poems by John Clare copyright © Eric Robinson 1997

Copyright in the unpublished and in much of the published work of John Clare is owned by Professor Eric Robinson who has together with the Oxford University Press authorised this publication.

The editor is grateful to Professor Robinson not only for allowing use of his texts but also for generously providing photocopies of unpublished texts, and offering helpful comment on the final version. Modifications of his authoritative texts are, however, the responsibility of the editor.

J. M. Dent
Orion Publishing Group
Orion House
5 Upper St Martin's Lane
London WC2H 9EA

Typeset by Deltatype Ltd, Birkenhead, Merseyside
Printed in Great Britain by
The Guernsey Press Co. Ltd., Guernsey, C. I.

British Library Cataloguing-in-Publication Data
is available upon request.

ISBN 0 460 87823 9

Contents

Birds and Beasts

Love

Loss and the Politics of Nature

John Clare, Poet

Note on the Author and Editor

JOHN CLARE was born on 13 July 1793 in the Northamptonshire village of Helpston. His father's knowledge of song was significantly wide, though his reading went little beyond the Bible; his mother's reading went scarcely so far. Clare, however, had an appetite for learning which ensured that he made the best use of all the teaching his parents could afford, and he read voraciously. When he was thirteen, he was set on his path to be a poet by discovering Thomson's *Seasons*, which inspired him to write down his first poem. He tried a number of jobs: ploughboy, gardener, helper at the local inn, lime-burner; he even joined the militia for a brief spell. His poems accumulated and, through contact with a local bookseller, he succeeded in having a book of poems published by Keats's publisher, John Taylor. His *Poems Descriptive of Rural Life and Scenery* (1820) went into four editions and was a success never to be repeated in spite of the quality of his three other books, *The Village Minstrel* (1821), *The Shepherd's Calendar* (1827) and *The Rural Muse* (1835). He married Patty Turner in 1820, not Mary Joyce, the childhood sweetheart and virtual muse to whom he always felt equally married. Clare struggled to reconcile contradictory expectations that he should be both working peasant and sophisticated poet. His general health was often weak and his mental condition declined. He was sent to an asylum in Epping Forest in 1837, from which he made a remarkable escape to his own village in 1841. He was committed to Northampton General Asylum, where he continued to write poetry. He died there on 20 May 1864.

R. K. R. THORNTON is Professor of English at the University of Birmingham. He has written on Hopkins and on *The Decadent Dilemma* (1983). He has edited Ivor Gurney, Nicholas Hilliard, the poets of the 1890s, John Clare's *The Midsummer Cushion* and *The Rural Muse* and most recently co-edited a 27-volume series of *Decadents, Symbolists, Anti-Decadents*.

Chronology of Clare's Life

Year	Life
1793	John Clare born on 13 July 1793 in the village of Helpston (at the time it had a final 'e'), then in Northamptonshire, first child and only son of Parker and Ann Clare. His twin sister, apparently the stronger child, dies. Clare's mother, Ann, was the daughter of John Stimson, the town shepherd of Castor; and his father Parker Clare, a thresher, was the illegitimate son of an itinerant Scottish schoolmaster, John Donald Parker
1797	Birth of Mary Joyce
1799	Birth of Martha Turner
1798–1806	Attends a Dame School in the village run by Mrs Bullimore, then a Vestry School in Glinton, where he is taught by Mr Seaton, later in a night school run by Mr Merrishaw. At Glinton he meets and falls in love with Mary Joyce, the woman who becomes his idealised love, his 'second wife' and in effect his muse
1806	Works as ploughboy for Mrs Bellairs of Woodcroft Castle. Buys James Thomson's *The Seasons* and writes down a poem for the first time: 'The Evening Walk'
c. 1807	Apprentice gardener at Burghley House
1809	Passing of the Act of Parliament for the enclosure of land which included the Helpston area. Working for Francis Gregory at the Blue Bell, the pub next door to his home
1812	Enlists in the Eastern Regiment of the Northamptonshire Local Militia, a reserve force behind the regular army and the regular militia. Clare volunteers, but only because the choice is either volunteering and receiving a bounty of £2 or being eligible for recruitment by ballot, which involves no bounty. The enlistment is for four years and service involves annual training, which we know Clare did in May/June 1812 and May/June 1813, and we know he was summoned to attend again in February 1814

Year	Life
1814	Buys blank book from J. B. Henson, a Market Deeping bookseller, an early adviser to Clare on his poetic aspirations
c. 1816	End of relationship with Mary Joyce, probably because of pressure from her family
1816–17	Working as gardener at Burghley House
1817	Working as lime-burner at Bridge Casterton. Meets Martha (Patty) Turner, who would become his wife
1818	Prospectus printed by Henson for a volume of poems by Clare to be published by subscription. Beginnings of association with Edward Drury, a Stamford bookseller
1819	First meets Isaiah Knowles Holland, a Congregational minister from Market Deeping and 'the first Encourager of My Obscure productions', and Octavius Gilchrist, a Stamford grocer, editor of *Drakard's Stamford News* who becomes a good friend of Clare. Drury introduces Clare to his cousin John Taylor, the London publisher (of Keats among others), who arranges to publish Clare's first volume. Earl Spencer grants Clare an annuity of £10
1820	On 16 January, *Poems Descriptive of Rural Life and Scenery* published by Taylor and Hessey of Fleet Street and E. Drury of Stamford. In February visits Milton Park, the residence of Lord Fitzwilliam. Visits Burghley House, the seat of the Marquis of Exeter, who grants him 15 guineas a year for life. In March he visits London with Gilchrist. Meets Lord Radstock, Mrs Emmerson, H. F. Cary (the translator of Dante), De Wint. His portrait is painted by William Hilton. On 16 March marries Martha (Patty) Turner at Casterton Magna. Records his first 'fit or rather swooning'. First child, Anna Maria, born on 2 June. A fund of £375 is collected for Clare and invested; annuities increase his yearly income to £43.15s
1821	January sees the fourth edition of *Poems Descriptive*. In May, Taylor takes over *The London Magazine* for which Clare writes from time to time. In May Clare writes an autobiographical sketch. 20 June: birth of a son who does not survive. In September, *The Village Minstrel, and other Poems* is published by Taylor and Hessey and E. Drury. Taylor visits Clare in Helpstone

Year	Life
1822	Second visit to London (May and June). Meets Lamb, Rippingille the painter, Hazlitt, Hood. A daughter, Eliza Louisa, born on 13 June
1822–5	Clare frequently very ill
1823	Finishes *The Parish*, which remains unpublished in his lifetime. 'Second edition' of *The Village Minstrel*. Gilchrist dies in June. Taylor suggests the subject of *The Shepherd's Calendar* in August and plans go ahead
1824	Birth of son, Frederick, on 5 January. Third visit to London (May to August). Meets Coleridge and De Quincey. On 14 July sees Byron's cortège on its way through London and is deeply impressed. Begins his Journal
1826	Birth of son, John, on 16 June
1827	*The Shepherd's Calendar, with Village Stories and Other Poems* published for Taylor by James Duncan; slow and poor sale
1828	Fourth visit to London (February). Treated by Dr Darling. Birth of son, William Parker, on 29 April
1830	Birth of daughter, Sophia, on 24 July. On 14 July, goes with the wife of the Bishop of Peterborough to a performance of *The Merchant of Venice* in Peterborough and publicly curses Shylock. Period of severe illnesses and possible breakdown
1831	Starts to transcribe poems for a projected volume to be called *The Midsummer Cushion*. Frustrations and setbacks before the eventual appearance in its place of a more modest selection, *The Rural Muse* (1835), from related manuscript
1832	Moves in June from the cottage in which he was born to a cottage in Northborough, three miles away, provided by Earl Fitzwilliam (see 'The Flitting')
1833	Birth of son, Charles, on 4 January
1835	Birth and death of an unnamed child. Clare awarded £50 from the Royal Literary Fund. In July, *The Rural Muse* published by Whittaker and Co. Clare's mother dies in December
1837	In June, Clare taken to Matthew Allen's Asylum at High Beech, Epping Forest. Regains some of his physical health

Year	*Life*
1838	In July, Mary Joyce, who had never married, dies aged 41
1841	Escapes from High Beech in July and walks the eighty miles back to Northborough in four days with little money or food, a journey recorded in his 'Journey out of Essex'. On December 29 he is taken to Northampton General Lunatic Asylum, where he spends the rest of his life. The notorious certificate of application for admission to Northampton General Lunatic Asylum records his usual employment as gardening, suggests his problems are hereditary and, to the question 'Was it [the insanity] preceded by any severe or long continued mental emotion or exertion?' answers 'after years addicted to Poetical prosings'
1843	Death of his son Frederick
1844	Death of daughter Anna Maria
1845	W. F. Knight begins collecting and transcribing poems written by Clare in the asylum, which he continues until his departure for Birmingham in 1850
1846	Death of Clare's father
1852	Death of son Charles
1864	Dies in Northampton, 20 May. Body taken (ironically, since it was the only rail journey he ever made) by train to Helpstone. Buried in the churchyard at Helpstone on 25 May

Introduction

Brief introductions to John Clare are likely to leave the reader with a caricature, rather than a convincing picture of the complex and interesting poet and writer that he was. Right from the time he and his publisher presented him in his first volume of poems as the 'Northamptonshire Peasant', there has been a tendency to undervalue his achievement by viewing him simply as a naive recorder of the countryside. There are two inscriptions in stone which are meant to honour the memory of John Clare, but epitomise this limitation: one is the memorial plaque in Poets' Corner in Westminster Abbey; the other is his tombstone in the churchyard of St Botolph's Church in Helpston, where he is buried.

The inscription in Westminster Abbey quotes one of Clare's lines: 'Fields were the essence of his song'. Of course, Clare was a remarkably close observer and accurate describer of the natural world; in a memorable phrase, James Fisher called him 'the finest poet of Britain's minor naturalists and the finest naturalist of Britain's major poets'. Almost any of the poems describing nature will indicate the remarkable knowledge he had of subtle details of plant and animal behaviour and natural change. For example, he is the only poet I know of who would be able to describe the changes in trees not by descriptions of the leaves, not by accounts of the blossom or berries, but by describing changes in the bark, as he does in 'Pleasures of Spring':

> The bark of trees puts gayer liveries on
> And varied hues through woodland thickets run:
> The blackthorn deepens in a darker stain
> And brighter freckles hazel shoots regain;
> The woodland rose in bright array is seen
> Whose bark receives like leaves a vivid green
> And foulroyce twigs as red as stockdoves' claws
> Shines in the woods to gain the bard's applause.

(In passing, notice the way the dialect – 'foulroyce' for dogwood and the use of a plural subject with the singular form of the verb –

reinforce the sense of rootedness in a place, with its specific identity of flora, fauna, customs and language.) But to limit Clare to a versifying naturalist is to fail to see his passionate concern for life in all its aspects. He is conscious of the changes happening not only in the countryside but in the whole life of the people, and he works to make permanent in his verse the things which he saw in danger of being forgotten or abandoned. He could see the changes that were happening in society; he could see the loss of country song and country customs, and he made a significant collection of folk song and folk music, probably the first in southern England (see George Deacon's *John Clare and the Folk Tradition*, Sinclair Browne, London, 1983, p. 18). The ways of a village (a projected title of one of his volumes) were dear to him – although his poetry made him something of an outsider – and customs, characters and modes of behaviour find a place in his verse as an intrinsic part of the countryside in which he lived. He is also, and significantly, a poet of love, perhaps equalled only by Burns (he was certainly influenced by Burns) in the lyric sweetness of his songs of the pleasures and pains of love. He is a fine satirist, however much he may have been subject to pressures not to publish satires like 'The Parish' while he lived; and he finds ways of addressing the politics of ecology in poems like 'The Moors', 'The Lament of Swordy Well' and 'The Fallen Elm'. Behind all these, and most impressively, he is a poet who is conscious of the way in which all his ideas are grounded in an idea of eternity. Eternity, an Eden of the imagination, is realised in certain aspects of existence which connect the world of experience to the world of permanence and truth; most important of these aspects are nature, love, childhood and poetry. He consciously works to identify their complex interrelationship, however much this is disguised in his apparent – but very artful – simplicity.

The second inscription, on Clare's gravestone, gives him little credit for his achievement. It memorialises him as 'The Northamptonshire Peasant Poet' and balances this description with the tag 'A poet is born not made'. Obviously something in his native make-up inclined him towards verse, but the achievement of his deceptively natural ease in poetry was the work of intense and persistent curiosity about all sorts of knowledge, including the nature and detail of experience and the business of poetry. Cicero said that we are born poets whereas we make ourselves orators. The fanciful idea of the well-educated that excellence in poetry should somehow be a gift when it occurs in those less formally educated was seized on by Renaissance writers. This is why Milton praises Shakespeare in 'L'Allegro' for 'Warbl[ing] his native wood-notes wild', and contrasts him to the learned Jonson. But Jonson, who knew Shakespeare and loved him 'on this side idolatry', argued in his lines on Shakespeare that 'a good poet's made, as well as born'. Clare, by strenuous learning and obsessive practice, made himself. He is undervalued if we are so foolish as to take him at his word when he over-modestly describes in 'Sighing for Retirement' how

> I found the poems in the fields,
> And only wrote them down.

Dr Nesbitt, who took over the running of the Northampton Asylum after Dr Prichard left, described to Frederick Martin, Clare's early biographer, how, when Clare was asked 'how he had contrived to write his pretty poetry', he replied that 'he kicked it out of the clods'. This fiction of the simple identity of poetry and nature is one that Clare likes to repeat. He expresses it succinctly in the way he uses the same word, 'poesy', for both a bunch of flowers and a group of poems. In 'Shadows of Taste' he argues that poetry can *be* nature but improve on it by being permanent:

> A blossom in its witchery of bloom,
> There gathered, dwells in beauty and perfume.
> The singing bird, the brook that laughs along
> There ceaseless sing and never thirsts for song.
> A pleasing image to its page conferred
> In living character and breathing word
> Becomes a landscape heard and felt and seen.

What Clare does not acknowledge here is the poetical skill by which he achieves this fixing of nature. His poetry is not a simple catalogue of the items composing a scene – he does not compose the scene in the formal ways of his eighteenth-century pastoral masters, though he learned from them – but a new way of seeing the movement between the simple and the vastly significant. Perhaps the clearest expression of this is in 'Song's Eternity', where he sees the apparently trivial song of the bluecap as 'Nature's universal tongue'. But it is there in his conviction of the transforming nature of love, in the imaginative conviction of childhood and in the power of poetry. If I had been able to choose an inscription for Poets' Corner, it would have been a line from the last stanza of 'Song's Eternity': 'Songs like the grass are evergreen', which suggests how poetry and the simple elements of nature are common and eternal.

These comments will help to explain my selection and the organisation of the poems. I have envisaged my reader as someone new to Clare and sampling what Clare has to offer before (I hope) being fascinated and looking further in his work. There are some practical difficulties in making a selection. Clare achieved his effects by accumulation and often accumulation at some length, and as a good countryman he loved stories; it has not been possible to represent this aspect of his work by selecting poems like 'Childhood' for example, or one of his long narratives. The selection is too short to allow for a significant representation of chronological development, though it is fair to say that in general I have chosen poems from the middle and later periods of Clare's life. I have tried to include the poems a reader familiar with Clare would expect to find, as well as some that are not so well known, but there are many which I have had to omit which seem as good as the ones I include. Clare is rather like Hardy in having a mass of poems from which few stand out but which all have value.

I have arranged the poems by theme rather than date of writing. I begin with a group of poems which deal with the country and the seasons and with the life of the village within that context. The second group is of poems on birds and beasts which not only indicate his close naturalist's observation, but also hint how he makes his birds and animals representative without being anthropomorphic. His interest in nests and the security of the individual bird in the face of the world's dangers is characteristic. I have chosen a group of poems of love in many of its forms, from first love, to painful feelings in love, to a sense of love's permanence. The next group – poems about loss and the threat of dispossession – should perhaps be in two sections, but I wished to emphasise the way in which his sense of his own identity was intimately connected with a sense of the integrity of nature and the rights of the individual within nature, threatened by the hateful changes taking place in the landscape, particularly through enclosure. I have ended with a selection of poems in which he examines himself and the way in which his poetry creates that self, and indeed creates or perceives the self of the world.

It is not only the selection of the poems which has exercised me somewhat, but also how to present them. When Clare was first published by John Taylor, it was expected that his poems would conform to the conventions of the time in regard to spelling and punctuation, and he left this largely in Taylor's hands. At times this seemed to be something that he wanted; he wrote to Taylor of the proofs of the second book that 'you will see I approve of every thing or nearly which you have done' (*The Letters of John Clare*, ed. Mark Storey, Clarendon Press, Oxford, 1985, p. 146). But there are other times when he seems to feel that the impositions of these conventions are damaging, as indeed they are, especially when they go so far as to try to 'correct' Clare's dialect. It is true that punctuation is surprisingly unnecessary, since the verse rhythm and the poetic line provide the punctuation for the ear. Clare wrote in his Journal that 'Editors are troubled with nice amendings and if Doctors were as fond of Amputation as they are of altering and correcting the world would have nothing but cripples' (*John Clare By Himself*, ed. Eric Robinson and David Powell, MidNAG and Carcanet, Ashington and Manchester, 1996, p. 225). Modern editors have trusted Clare and gone back to his manuscripts, and the best editions will print Clare's writings exactly as he wrote them, with his private spelling schemes ('hugh' for 'huge', 'piegons' for 'pigeons' for example), with minimal punctuation, and with no alteration of his dialect, either in vocabulary or in grammar. Clare felt he had Cobbett's support in writing that 'what ever is intelligible to others is grammer and what ever is commonsense is not far from correctness' (*The Oxford Authors John Clare*, Oxford University Press, 1984, p. 481). In a letter he wrote that 'grammar in learning is like tyranny in government – confound the bitch I'll never be her slave' (*Letters*, p. 231). Despite this, it seems to me that a new reader of Clare may well be initially put off by unconventional spellings of words, and the enjoyment of Clare's lines interrupted by some puzzlement about the direction of the grammar. Since there are now such dependable basic texts which reproduce Clare, I felt it was time to take away any initial strangeness for the new reader. I have therefore standardised most spellings; I say most because when a spelling is an integral part of the rhyme, it would destroy the rhyme to change it. I have not altered Clare's dialect words and dialect forms (such as the plural 'childern'), and I have provided a glossary of what seem to be the puzzling ones; and I have not normalised

Clare's grammar, of which a particularly noticeable feature is the non-agreement of subject and verb: this was quite normal for his place and day. In punctuating, I have been very much aware that punctuation places some restrictions on Clare's meanings. His sentences often move with a seamless ease; an exact grammatical relationship is perhaps deliberately avoided. The best punctuation mark often seemed to be the dash which Emily Dickinson found so useful. I have punctuated sparingly, but I hope enough to allow Clare to speak for himself without the damaging caricature of the 'unlettered poet'. His various and vivid qualities the poems themselves will show.

R. K. R. THORNTON

John Clare

A Country Village Year

December from 'The Shepherd's Calendar'

CHRISTMAS

Christmas is come and every hearth
Makes room to give him welcome now.
E'en want will dry its tears in mirth
And crown him wi' a holly bough,
Though tramping 'neath a Winter sky
O'er snow track paths and rimey stiles.
The huswife sets her spinning by
And bids him welcome wi' her smiles.

Each house is swept the day before
And windows stuck wi' evergreens,
The snow is besomed from the door
And comfort crowns the cottage scenes.
Gilt holly wi' its thorny pricks
And yew and box wi' berries small,
These deck the unused candlesticks
And pictures hanging by the wall.

Neighbours resume their annual cheer,
Wishing wi' smiles and spirits high
Glad Christmas and a happy year
To every morning passer by.
Milk maids their Christmas journeys go
Accompanied wi' favoured swain
And childern pace the crumping snow
To taste their granny's cake again.

Hung wi' the ivy's veining bough
The ash trees round the cottage farm
Are often stripped of branches now

The cotter's Christmas hearth to warm.
He swings and twists his hazel band
And lops them off wi' sharpened hook
And oft brings ivy in his hand
To decorate the chimney nook.

Old Winter wipes his icles by
And warms his fingers till he smiles
Where cottage hearths are blazing high
And labour resteth from his toils;
Wi' merry mirth beguiling care,
Old customs keeping wi' the day,
Friends meet their Christmas cheer to share
And pass it in a harmless way.

Old customs, O I love the sound,
However simple they may be;
Whate'er wi' time has sanction found
Is welcome and is dear to me.
Pride grows above simplicity
And spurns it from her haughty mind
And soon the poet's song will be
The only refuge they can find.

The shepherd now no more afraid,
Since custom doth the chance bestow,
Starts up to kiss the giggling maid
Beneath the branch of mistletoe
That neath each cottage beam is seen
Wi' pear-like-berries shining gay,
The shadow still of what hath been
Which fashion yearly fades away.

And singers too, a merry throng,
At early morn wi' simple skill
Yet imitate the angels' song
And chant their Christmas ditty still;
And mid the storm that dies and swells
By fits – in hummings softly steals

The music of the village bells
Ringing round their merry peals.

And when it's past, a merry crew
Bedecked in masks and ribbons gay
The 'Morris dance' their sports renew
And act their Winter evening play.
The clown-turned-kings for penny praise
Storm wi' the actor's strut and swell
And harlequin a laugh to raise
Wears his hump back and tinkling bell.

And oft for pence and spicy ale
Wi' Winter nosegays pinned before
The wassail singer tells her tale
And drawls her Christmas carols o'er.
The prentice boy wi' ruddy face
And rime-bepowdered dancing locks
From door to door wi' happy pace
Runs round to claim his 'Christmas box'.

The block behind the fire is put
To sanction custom's old desires,
And many a faggot's bands are cut
For the old farmer's Christmas fires,
Where loud-tongued gladness joins the throng
And Winter meets the warmth of May,
Feeling betimes the heat too strong
And rubs his shins and draws away.

While snows the window panes bedim
The fire curls up, a sunny charm,
Where creaming o'er the pitcher's rim
The flowering ale is set to warm.
Mirth full of joy as Summer bees
Sits there its pleasures to impart
While childern 'tween their parents' knees
Sing scraps of carols o'er by heart.

And some to view the Winter weathers
Climb up the window seat wi' glee,

Likening the snow to falling feathers
In fancy's infant ecstasy,
Laughing wi' superstition's love
O'er visions wild that youth supplies
Of people pulling geese above
And keeping Christmas in the skies.

As though the homestead trees were dressed
In lieu of snow wi' dancing leaves,
As though the sun-dried martin's nest
Instead of icles hung the eaves,
The childern hail the happy day
As if the snow was April grass
And pleased as 'neath the warmth of May
Sport o'er the water froze to glass.

Thou day of happy sound and mirth
That long wi' childish memory stays,
How blessed around the cottage hearth
I met thee in my boyish days,
Harping wi' rapture's dreaming joys
O'er presents that thy coming found,
The welcome sight of little toys,
The Christmas gifts of comers-round:

The wooden horse wi' arching head
Drawn upon wheels around the room,
The gilded coach of ginger bread
And many-coloured sugar plum;
Gilt-covered books for pictures sought
Or stories childhood loves to tell,
Wi' many an urgent promise bought
To get tomorrow's lesson well;

And many a thing a minute's sport
Left broken on the sanded floor
When we would leave our play and court
Our parents' promises for more,

Though manhood bids such raptures die
And throws such toys away as vain,
Yet memory loves to turn her eye
And talk such pleasures o'er again.

Around the glowing hearth at night
The harmless laugh and Winter tale
Goes round – while parting friends delight
To toast each other o'er their ale.
The cotter oft wi' quiet zeal
Will musing o'er his Bible lean
While in the dark the lovers steal
To kiss and toy behind the screen.

The yule cake dotted thick wi' plums
Is on each supper table found,
And cats look up for falling crumbs
Which greedy childern litter round,
And huswife's sage-stuffed seasoned chine
Long hung in chimney nook to dry
And boiling elder berry wine
To drink the Christmas eve's 'Goodbye'.

Sonnet: 'The barn door is open'

The barn door is open and ready to winnow,
The woodman is resting and getting his dinner
And calls to the maiden with little to say
Who takes the hot dinner and hurries away.
The hen's in the dust and the hog's in the dirt,
The mower is busy and stripped in his shirt,
The waggon is empty and ready to start,
The ploughman is merry and drinking his quart,
The men are at work and the schoolboy at play,

The maid's in the meadow a-making the hay;
The ducks are a feeding and running about,
The hogs are a-noising and try to get out;
The dog's at his bone and the ass at his tether,
And cows in the pasture all feeding together.

The Wheat Ripening

What time the wheat field tinges rusty brown
And barley bleaches in its mellow grey,
'Tis sweet some smooth-mown balk to wander down
Or cross the fields on footpath's narrow way
Just in the mealy light of waking day
As glittering dewdrops moise the maiden's gown
And sparkling bounces from her nimble feet
Journeying to milking from the neighbouring town
Making life light with song – and it is sweet
To mark the grazing herds and list the clown
Urge on his ploughing team with cheering calls
And merry shepherd's whistling toils begun
And hoarse-tongued birdboy whose unceasing calls
Join the lark's ditty to the rising sun.

The Beans in Blossom

The southwest wind, how pleasant in the face
It breathes while, sauntering in a musing pace,
I roam these new-ploughed fields and by the side
Of this old wood where happy birds abide
And the rich blackbird through his golden bill
Utters wild music when the rest are still.
Now luscious comes the scent of blossomed beans

That o'er the path in rich disorder leans,
'Mid which the bees in busy songs and toils
Load home luxuriantly their yellow spoils.
The herd cows toss the mole hills in their play
And often stand the stranger's steps at bay,
'Mid clover blossoms red and tawny white,
Strong scented with the Summer's warm delight.

Sonnet: 'The landscape laughs in Spring'

The landscape laughs in Spring and stretches on
Its growing distance of refreshing dyes.
From pewit-haunted flats the floods are gone
And like a carpet the green meadow lies
In merry hues and edged wi' yellow flowers.
The trickling brook veins sparkling to the sun
Like to young may-flies dancing wi' the hours.
The noising childern 'mid the young grass run,
Gathering wi' village dames from balk and lea
The swarming cowslips wi' commingling play
To make praise-worthy wine and savoury tea,
And drink a Winter memory of May
When all the season's joys have ceased to be
And flowers and sunny hours have passed away.

Sonnet: 'I dreaded walking
where there was no path'

I dreaded walking where there was no path
And pressed with cautious tread the meadow swath
And always turned to look with wary eye
And always feared the owner coming by;

Yet everything about where I had gone
Appeared so beautiful I ventured on
And when I gained the road where all are free
I fancied every stranger frowned at me
And every kinder look appeared to say
You've been on trespass in your walk today.
I've often thought the day appeared so fine,
How beautiful if such a place were mine;
But having nought I never feel alone
And cannot use another's as my own.

Sonnet: 'The passing traveller'

The passing traveller with wonder sees
A deep and ancient stone pit full of trees,
So deep and very deep the place has been
The church might stand within and not be seen.
The passing stranger oft with wonder stops
And thinks he e'en could walk upon their tops
And often stoops to see the busy crow
And stands above and sees the eggs below;
And while the wild horse gives his head a toss
The squirrel dances up and runs across.
The boy that stands and kills the black-nosed bee
Dares down as soon as magpies' nests are found
And wonders when he climbs the highest tree
To find it reaches scarce above the ground.

Sport in the Meadows

Maytime is to the meadows coming in
And cowslip peeps have gotten e'er so big
And water-blobs and all their golden kin
Crowd round the shallows by the striding brig.
Daisies and buttercups and lady-smocks
Are all abouten shining here and there,
Nodding about their gold and yellow locks
Like morts of folken flocking at a fair.
The sheep and cows are crowding for a share
And snatch the blossoms in such eager haste
That basket-bearing childern running there
Do think within their hearts they'll get them all
And hoot and drive them from their graceless waste
As though there wa'n't a cowslip peep to spare
– For they want some for tea and some for wine
And some to maken up a cuckaball
To throw across the garland's silken line
That reaches o'er the street from wall to wall
– Good gracious me, how merrily they fare.
One sees a fairer cowslip than the rest
And off they shout – the foremost bidding fair
To get the prize – and earnest half and jest
The next one pops her down – and from her hand
Her basket falls and out her cowslips all
Tumble and litter there – the merry band
In laughing friendship round about her fall
To helpen gather up the littered flowers
That she no less may mourn – and now the wind
In frolic mood among the merry hours
Wakens with sudden start and tosses off
Some untied bonnet on its dancing wings.
Away they follow with a scream and laugh
And aye the youngest ever lags behind
Till on the deep lake's very brink it hings.
They shout and catch it and then off they start
To chase for cowslips merry as before;
And each one seems so anxious at the heart

As they would even get them all and more.
One climbs a molehill for a bunch of May,
One stands on tiptoe for a linnet's nest
And pricks her hand and throws her flowers away
And runs for plantain leaves to have it dressed.
So do they run abouten all the day
And tease the grass-hid larks from getting rest
– Scarce give they time in their unruly haste
To tie a shoestring that the grass unties,
And thus they run the meadow's bloom to waste
Till even comes and dulls their phantasies,
When one finds losses out to stifle smiles
Of silken bonnet strings – and others sigh
O'er garments renten clambering over stiles.
Yet in the morning fresh afield they hie
Bidding the last day's troubles all goodbye,
When red-pied cow again their coming hears
And, ere they clap the gate, she tosses up
Her head and hastens from the sport she fears;
The old ewe calls her lamb nor cares to stoop
To crop a cowslip in their company.
Thus merrily the little noisy troop
Along the grass as rude marauders hie
For ever noisy and forever gay
While keeping in the meadows holiday.

Emmonsales Heath

In thy wild garb of other times
I find thee lingering still;
Furze o'er each lazy summit climbs
At nature's easy will;

Grasses that never knew a scythe
Waves all the summer long

And wild weed-blossoms waken blythe
That ploughshares never wrong.

Stern industry with stubborn pride
And wants unsatisfied
Still leaves untouched thy maiden soil
In its unsullied pride.

The birds still find their summer shade
To build their nests again
And the poor hare its rushy glade
To hide from savage men.

Nature its family protects
In thy security
And blooms that love what man neglects
Find peaceful homes in thee.

The wild rose scents thy summer air
And woodbines weave in bowers
To glad the swain sojourning there
And maidens gathering flowers.

Creation's steps one's wandering meets
Untouched by those of man;
Things seem the same in such retreats
As when the world began.

Furze, ling and brake all mingling free
And grass forever green
All seem the same old things to be
As they have ever been.

The brook o'er such neglected ground
One's weariness to soothe
Still wildly threads its lawless bounds
And chafes the pebble smooth,

Crooked and rude as when at first
Its waters learned to stray

And, from their mossy fountain burst,
It washed itself a way.

O who can pass such lovely spots
Without a wish to stray
And leave life's cares a while forgot
To muse an hour away?

I've often met with places rude
Nor failed their sweet to share
But passed an hour with solitude
And left my blessing there.

He that can meet the morning wind
And o'er such places roam
Nor leave a lingering wish behind
To make their peace his home,

His heart is dead to quiet hours,
No love his mind employs;
Poesy with him ne'er shares its flowers
Nor solitude its joys.

O there are spots amid thy bowers
Which nature loves to find,
Where Spring drops round her earliest flowers
Unchecked by Winter's wind,

Where cowslips wake the child's surprise
Sweet peeping ere their time,
Ere April spreads her dappled skies
'Mid morning's powdered rime.

I've stretched my boyish walks to thee
When Mayday's paths were dry,
When leaves had nearly hid each tree
And grass greened ankle high,

And mused the sunny hours away
And thought of little things

That childern mutter o'er their play
When fancy tries its wings.

Joy nursed me in her happy moods
And all life's little crowd
That haunt the waters, fields and woods
Would sing their joys aloud.

I thought how kind that mighty power
Must in his splendour be
Who spread around my boyish hour
Such gleams of harmony,

Who did with joyous rapture fill
The low as well as high
And made the pismires round the hill
Seem full as blest as I.

Hope's sun is seen of every eye;
The halo that it gives
In nature's wide and common sky
Cheers every thing that lives.

Summer Tints

How sweet I've wandered bosom-deep in grain
When Summer's mellowing pencil sweeps his shades
Of ripening tinges o'er the checkered plain:
Light tawny oat-lands wi' their yellow blades
And bearded corn like armies on parade,
Beans lightly scorched that still preserved their green
And nodding lands of wheat in bleachy brown
And streaking banks where many a maid and clown
Contrasts a sweetness to the rural scene,
Forming the little haycocks up and down,
While o'er the face of nature softly swept
The lingering wind mixing the brown and green,

So sweet that shepherds from their bowers have crept
And stood delighted musing o'er the scene.

The Summer Shower

I love it well o'ercanopied in leaves
Of crowding woods to spend a quiet hour
And where the woodbine weaves
To list the summer shower,

Brought by the south west wind that balm and bland
Breathes luscious coolness loved and felt by all,
While on the uplifted hand
The rain drops gently fall.

Now quickening on and on, the pattering woods
Receives the coming shower, birds trim their wings
And in a joyful mood
The little woodchat sings,

And blackbird squatting on her mortared nest
Safe hid in ivy and the pathless wood
Pruneth her sooty breast
And warms her downy brood;

And little Pettichap like hurrying mouse
Keeps nimbling near my arbour round and round.
Aye, there's her oven house
Built nearly on the ground

Of wood-bents, withered straws and moss and leaves
And lined with downy feathers. Safety's joy
Dwells with the home she weaves
Nor fears the pilfering boy.

The busy falling rain increases now
And sopping leaves their dripping moisture pour

And from each loaded bough
Fast falls the double shower.

Weed climbing hedges, banks and meeds unmown
Where rushy-fringed brooklet easy curls
Look joyous while the rain
Strings their green suit with pearls,

While from the crouching corn the weeding troop
Run hastily and, huddling in a ring
Where the old willows stoop,
Their ancient ballads sing

And gabble over wonder's ceaseless tale,
Till from the southwest sky showers thicker come
Humming along the vale
And bids them hasten home.

With laughing skip they stride the hasty brook
That mutters through the weeds until it gains
A clear and quiet nook
To greet the dimpling rain,

And on they drabble all in mirth not mute,
Leaving their footmarks on the elting soil
Where print of sprawling foot
Stirs up a tittering smile

On beauty's lips who, slipping 'mid the crowd,
Blushes to have her ankle seen so high
Yet inly feeleth proud
That none a fault can spy;

Yet rudely followed by the meddling clown
Who passes vulgar gibes – the bashful maid
Lets go her folded gown
And pauses half afraid

To climb the stile before him till the dame,
To quarrel half provoked, assails the knave

And laughs him into shame
And makes him well behave.

Birdnesting boys o'ertaken in the rain
Beneath the ivied maple bustling run
And wait in anxious pain
Impatient for the sun

And sigh for home, yet at the pasture gate
The molehill-tossing bull with straining eye
Seemeth their steps to wait
Nor dare they pass him by

Till, wearied out, high over hedge they scrawl
To shun the road and through the wet grass roam
Till wet and draggled all
They fear to venture home.

The plough team wet and dripping plashes home
And on the horse the ploughboy lolls along
Yet from the wet grounds come
The loud and merry song.

Now 'neath the leafy arch of dripping bough
That loaded trees form o'er the narrow lane
The horse released from plough
Naps the moist grass again.

Around their blanket camps the gipsies still
Heedless of showers while blackthorns shelter round
Jump o'er the pasture hills
In many an idle bound.

From dark green clumps among the dripping grain
The lark with sudden impulse starts and sings
And 'mid the smoking rain
Quivers her russet wings.

A joy-inspiring calmness all around
Breathes a refreshing sense of strengthening power

Like that which toil hath found
In Sunday's leisure hour

When spirits all relaxed, heartsick of toil,
Seeks out the pleasant woods and shadowy dells
And where the fountain boils
Lie listening distant bells.

Amid the yellow furze, the rabbit's bed,
Labour hath hid his tools and o'er the heath
Hies to the milking shed
That stands the oak beneath

And there he wiles the pleasant shower away
Filling his mind with store of happy things,
Rich crops of corn and hay
And all that plenty brings.

The cramped horizon now leans on the ground,
Quiet and cool, and labour's hard employ
Ceases while all around
Falls a refreshing joy.

Summer Moods

I love at eventide to walk alone
Down narrow lanes o'erhung with dewy thorn,
Where from the long grass underneath, the snail
Jet black creeps out and sprouts his timid horn.
I love to muse o'er meadows newly mown
Where withering grass perfumes the sultry air,
Where bees search round with sad and weary drone
In vain for flowers that bloomed but newly there,
While in the juicy corn the hidden quail
Cries 'wet my foot' and, hid as thoughts unborn,

The fairylike and seldom-seen landrail
Utters 'craik craik' like voices underground,
Right glad to meet the evening's dewy veil
And see the light fade into glooms around.

Sonnet: 'The maiden ran away'

The maiden ran away to fetch the clothes
And threw her apron o'er her cap and bows,
But the shower catched her ere she hurried in
And beat and almost dowsed her to the skin.
The ruts ran brooks as they would ne'er be dry
And the boy waded as he hurried by.
The half-drowned ploughman waded to the knees
And birds were almost drowned upon the trees.
The streets ran rivers till they floated o'er
And women screamed to meet it at the door.
Labour fled home and rivers hurried by
And still it fell as it would never stop.
E'en the old stone pit deep as house is high
Was brimming o'er and floated o'er the top.

Song: 'She tied up her few things'

She tied up her few things
And laced up her shoe strings
And put on her bonnet worn through at the crown;
Her apron tied tighter,
Than snow her caps whiter,
She lapped up her earnings and left our old town.

The Dog barked again
All the length o' his chain
And licked her hand kindly and huffed her goodbye;
Old hens prated loudly,
The Cock strutted proudly
And the horse at the gate turned to let her go by.

The Thrasher-man stopping
The old barn-floor whopping
Wished o'er the door-cloth her luck and no harm.
Bees hummed round the thistle
While the red Robins whistle
And she took just one look on the old mossy farm.

'Twas Michaelmas season;
They'd got corn and peas in
And all the fields cleared save some ruckings and tythes.
Cote-pigeon-flocks muster,
Round beans shelling cluster
And done are the whettings o' reap-hooks and scythes.

Next year's flowers a-springing
Will miss Jinney's singing.
She opened her Bible and turned a leaf down.
In her bosom's forewarnings
She lapped up her earnings
And ere the sun's set'll be in her own town.

The Foddering Boy

The foddering boy along the crumping snows
With straw-band-belted legs and folded arm
Hastens and on the blast that keenly blows
Oft turns for breath and beats his fingers warm
And shakes the lodging snows from off his clothes,
Buttoning his doublet closer from the storm
And slouching his brown beaver o'er his nose,

Then faces it again – and seeks the stack
Within its circling fence – where hungry lows
Expecting cattle making many a track
About the snows – impatient for the sound
When in huge fork-fulls trailing at his back
He litters the sweet hay about the ground
And brawls to call the staring cattle round.

The Gipsy Camp

The snow falls deep; the Forest lies alone:
The boy goes hasty for his load of brakes,
Then thinks upon the fire and hurries back;
The Gipsy knocks his hands and tucks them up,
And seeks his squalid camp, half hid in snow,
Beneath the oak, which breaks away the wind,
And bushes close, with snow like hovel warm:
There stinking mutton roasts upon the coals,
And the half-roasted dog squats close and rubs,
Then feels the heat too strong and goes aloof;
He watches well, but none a bit can spare,
And vainly waits the morsel thrown away:
'Tis thus they live – a picture to the place;
A quiet, pilfering, unprotected race.

Winter Fields

O for a pleasant book to cheat the sway
Of winter – where rich mirth with hearty laugh
Listens and rubs his legs on corner seat,
For fields are mire and sludge – and badly off
Are those who on their pudgy paths delay.

There striding shepherd seeking driest way,
Fearing night's wetshod feet and hacking cough
That keeps him waken till the peep of day,
Goes shouldering onward and with ready hook
Progs off to ford the sloughs that nearly meet
Across the lands – croodling and thin to view
His loath dog follows – stops and quakes and looks
For better roads – till whistled to pursue,
Then on with frequent jumps he hirkles through.

The Cottager

True as the church clock hand the hour pursues
He plods about his toils and reads the news,
And at the blacksmith's shop his hour will stand
To talk of 'Lunun' as a foreign land,
For from his cottage door in peace or strife
He ne'er went fifty miles in all his life.
His knowledge with old notions still combined
Is twenty years behind the march of mind;
He views new knowledge with suspicious eyes
And thinks it blasphemy to be so wise.
O'er steam's almighty tales he wondering looks
As witchcraft gleaned from old blackletter books.
Life gave him comfort but denied him wealth;
He toils in quiet and enjoys his health;
He smokes a pipe at night and drinks his beer
And runs no scores on tavern screens to clear.
He goes to market all the year about
And keeps one hour and never stays it out.
E'en at St Thomas-tide old Rover's bark
Hails Dapple's trot an hour before it's dark.
He is a simple-worded plain old man
Whose good intents take errors in their plan;
Oft sentimental and with saddened vein
He looks on trifles and bemoans their pain

And thinks the angler mad and loudly storms
With emphasis of speech o'er murdered worms
And hunters cruel – pleading with sad care
Pity's petition for the fox and hare;
Yet feels self-satisfaction in his woes
For war's crushed myriads of his slaughtered foes.
He is right scrupulous in one pretext
And wholesale errors swallows in the next.
He deems it sin to sing yet not to say
A song, a mighty difference in his way;
And many a moving tale in antique rhymes
He has for Christmas and such merry times
When 'Chevy Chase', his masterpiece of song,
Is said so earnest none can think it long.
'Twas the old Vicar's way, who should be right,
For the late Vicar was his heart's delight,
And while at church he often shakes his head
To think what sermons the old vicar made,
Downright orthodox, that all the land
Who had their ears to hear might understand.
But now such mighty learning meets his ears
He thinks it Greek or Latin which he hears.
Yet church receives him every sabbath day
And, rain or snow, he never keeps away.
All words of reverence still his heart reveres,
Low bows his head when Jesus meets his ears
And still he thinks it blasphemy as well
Such names without a capital to spell.
In an old corner cupboard by the wall
His books are laid – though good, in number small.
His Bible first in place – from worth and age,
Whose grandsire's name adorns the title page
And, blank leaves once, now filled with kindred claims
Display a world's epitome of names,
Parents and childern and grandchildern, all
Memory's affections in the lists recall.
And Prayer book next, much worn though strongly bound,
Proves him a churchman orthodox and sound.
The 'Pilgrims Progress' too and 'Death of Abel'

Are seldom missing from his reading table.
And prime old Tusser in his homely trim,
The first of bards in all the world with him
And only poet which his leisure knows
– Verse deals in fancy so he sticks to prose.
These are the books he reads and reads again
And weekly hunts the almanacs for rain.
Here and no further learning's channels ran;
Still neighbours prize him as the learned man.
His cottage is a humble place of rest
With one spare room to welcome every guest
And that tall poplar pointing to the sky
His own hand planted when an idle boy.
It shades his chimney while the singing wind
Hums songs of shelter to his happy mind.
Within his cot the 'largest ears of corn'
He ever found his picture frames adorn:
Brave Granby's head, De Grasse's grand defeat;
He rubs his hands and tells how Rodney beat.
And from the rafters upon strings depend
Beanstalks beset with pods from end to end
Whose numbers without counting may be seen
Wrote on the Almanac behind the screen.
Around the corner upon worsted strung
Pooties in wreaths above the cupboards hung;
Memory at trifling incidents awakes
And there he keeps them for his childern's sakes
Who when as boys searched every sedgy lane,
Traced every wood and shattered clothes again
Roaming about on rapture's easy wing
To hunt those very pooty shells in spring.
And thus he lives too happy to be poor
While strife ne'er pauses at so mean a door.
Low in the sheltered valley stands his cot;
He hears the mountain storm – and feels it not.
Winter and Spring toil ceasing ere 'tis dark,
Rests with the lamb and rises with the lark.
Content is helpmate to the day's employ

And care ne'er comes to steal a single joy.
Time scarcely noticed turns his hair to grey
Yet leaves him happy as a child at play.

The Crow Sat on the Willow

The crow sat on the willow tree
A-lifting up his wings
And glossy was his coat to see
And loud the ploughman sings:
'I love my love because I know
The milkmaid she loves me';
And hoarsely croaked the glossy crow
Upon the willow tree.
'I love my love', the ploughman sung
And all the field wi' music rung.

'I love my love, a bonny lass,
She keeps her pails so bright
And blythe she trips the dewy grass
At morning and at night;
A cotton drab her morning gown;
Her face was rosy health;
She traced the pastures up and down
And nature was her wealth'.
He sung and turned each furrow down;
His sweetheart's love in cotton gown.

'My love is young and handsome
As any in the town;
She's worth a ploughman's ransom
In the drab cotton gown',
He sung and turned his furrows o'er

And urged his team along,
While on the willow as before
The old crow croaked his song.
The ploughman sung his rustic lay
And sung of Phoebe all the day.

The crow was in love no doubt
And wi' a many things;
The ploughman finished many a bout
And lustily he sings,
'My love she is a milking maid
Wi' red and rosy cheek;
O' cotton drab her gown was made;
I loved her many a week'.
His milking maid the ploughman sung
Till all the fields around him rung.

from 'The Parish'

*'No injury can possibly be done, as a nameless character can
never be found out but by its truth and likeness'*: Pope

The Parish hind, oppression's humble slave,
Whose only hopes of freedom is the grave;
The cant miscalled religion in the saint
And Justice mocked while listening want's complaint;
The parish laws and parish queens and kings,
Pride's lowest classes of pretending things;
The meanest dregs of tyranny and crime,
I fearless sing; let truth attend the rhyme,
Though nowadays truth grows a vile offence
And courage tells it at his own expense;
If he but utter what himself has seen
He deals in satire and he wounds too keen,
Intends sly ruin by encroached degrees,

Is rogue or radical or what you please;
But should vile flatterers with the basest lies
Attempt self interest with a wished disguise,
Say groves of myrtle here in winter grow
And blasts blow blessings every time they blow,
That golden showers in mercy fall to bless
The half-thatched mouldering hovels of distress,
That Eden's self in freedom's infant sphere
Was but a desert to our Eden here,
That laws so wise to choke the seeds of strife
Here bless a beggar with an Adam's life,
Ah, what an host of Patronisers then
Would gather round the motley flatterer's den:
A spotted monster in a lambkin's hide,
Whose smooth tongue uttered what his heart denied.
They'd call his genius wondrous in extreme
And lisp the novel beauties of his theme
And say 'twas luck on nature's kinder part
To bless such genius with a gentle heart.
Cursed affectation, worse than hell I hate
Thy sheepish features and thy crouching gait,
Like sneaking cur that licks his master's shoe,
Bowing and cringing to the Lord knows who,
Licking the dust for each approving nod
Where pride is worshipped like an earthly god.
The rogue that's carted to the gallows tree
Is far more honest in his trade than thee.
Thy puling whine that suits thy means so well,
Piteous as chicken's breaking through its shell,
That rarely fails to ope the closest purse,
Is far more roguish than the other's force.
I dread no cavils, for the clearest sink,
Whene'er the bottom's stirred, is sure to stink.
So let them rail; I envy not their praise
Nor fear the slander stung deceit may raise.
Let those who merit what the verse declares
Choose to be vexed and think the picture theirs.
On Life's rude sea my bark is launched afar
And they may wish the wreck who dread the war;
Than waves in storms their spite is nothing more,

That lash rage weary on a heedless shore.
A public name's the shuttle-cock of fame,
Now up then down as fashion wills the game,
At whom each fool may cast his private lie
Nor fear the scourge of satire's just reply,
While those who rail may do what deeds they list;
They hide in ignorance and are never missed;
Their scorn is envy's imp conceived by hate
That tortures worth in every grade and state.
As mists today, as shadows to the sun,
These stains in merit's welfare ever run,
Diseases that infect not but at last
Die of their own distempers and are past.
Such friends I count not and such foes disdain;
Their best or worst is neither loss nor gain;
Friendship like theirs is but the name's disgrace,
A mask that counterfeits its open face.
Cant and hypocrisy disguise their ways,
Their praise turns satire and their satire praise.
Good men are ever from such charges free;
To prove them friends is praise enough for me.

Satire should not wax civil o'er its toil,
Tho sweet self-interest blossoms on the soil,
Nor like a barking dog betray its trust
By silence when the robber throws his crust,
Till fear and mercy all its wrath divides
To feeble portraits buttered on both sides.
I'll strive to do what flattery bids me shun,
Tell truth nor shrink for benefits to none;
Folly's a fool that cannot keep its ground,
Still fearing foes and shewing where to wound.
A jealous look will almost turn her sick
And hints not meant oft galls her to the quick;
And, hide or shuffle or do what she will,
Each mask like glass reflects the picture still.
As powder kindles from the smallest spark,
Confusion buzzes and betrays the mark.
From such frail sources every fact is drawn,

Not sought through malice or exposed in scorn
But told as truths that common sense may see
How cant's pretensions and her works agree.
I could not pass her low deceptions by
Nor can I flatter and I will not lie.
So satire's Muse shall like a bloodhound trace
Each smoothfaced tyrant to his hiding place,
Whose hidden actions, like the fox's skin,
Scents the sly track to where they harbour in;
And each profession of this Parish troop
Shall have a rally ere the hunt be up.
To none that rules I owe nor spite nor grudge;
How just the satire he who reads may judge.

   That good old fame the farmers earned of yore,
That made as equals, not as slaves, the poor,
That good old fame did in two sparks expire:
A shooting coxcomb and a hunting Squire;
And their old mansions that was dignified
With things far better than the pomp of pride,
At whose oak table that was plainly spread
Each guest was welcomed and the poor was fed;
Where master, son and serving-man and clown
Without distinction daily sat them down;
Where the bright rows of pewter by the wall
Served all the pomp of kitchen or of hall;
These all have vanished like a dream of good
And the slim things that rises where they stood
Are built by those whose clownish taste aspires
To hate their farms and ape the country squires.
The old oak table soon betook to flight,
A thing disgusting to my lady's sight.
Yet affectations of a tender claim
To the past memory of its owner's name,
Whose wealth, pride's only beauty, stood her friend
And bought a husband that same wealth to spend,
Laid it aside in lumber rooms to rot
Till, all past claims of tenderness forgot,

Bade it its honourable name resign,
Transformed to stable doors or troughs for swine.
Each aged labourer knows its history well
And sighs in sorrow like sad change to tell.
The pewter rows are all exchanged for plate
And that choice patch of pride to mark them great
Of red or blue, gay as an harlequin,
The liveried footman serves the dinner in,
As like the squire as pride can imitate,
Save that no porter watches at the gate;
And even his Lordship, thought so grand before,
Is but distinguished in his coach and four.
Such are the upstarts that usurp the name
Of the old farmer's dignity and fame;
And where's that lovely maid in days gone by,
The farmer's daughter, unreserved though shy,
That milked her cows and old songs used to sing
As red and rosy as the lovely spring?
Ah, these have dwindled to a formal shade
As pale and bed-rid as my lady's maid,
Who cannot dare to venture in the street,
Some times through cold, at other times for heat;
And, vulgar eyes to shun and vulgar winds,
Shrouded in veils green as their window blinds.
These, taught at school their stations to despise
And view old customs with disdainful eyes,
Deem all as rude their kindred did of yore
And scorn to toil or foul their fingers more;
Prim as the pasteboard figures which they cut
At school and tasteful on the chimney put,
They sit before their glasses hour by hour
Or paint unnatural daubs of fruit or flower,
Or, boasting learning, novels' beauties quotes
Or, aping fashions, scream a tune by notes.
E'en poetry in these high-polished days
Is oft profaned by their dislike or praise.
They've read the *Speaker* till without a look
They'll sing whole pages and lay by the book;

Then, sure, their judgment must be good indeed
Whene'er they choose to speak of what they read,
To simper tasteful some devoted line
As something bad or something very fine.
Thus mincing fine airs misconceived at school
That pride out-Herods and completes the fool;
Thus housed mid cocks and hens in idle state,
Aping at fashions which their betters hate,
Affecting high life's airs to scorn the past,
Trying to be something makes them nought at last.
These are the shadows that supply the place
Of farmers' daughters of the vanished race;
And what are these rude names will do them harm?
O rather call them 'Ladies of the Farm'.

Miss Peevish Scornful, once the Village toast,
Deemed fair by some and prettyish by most,
Brought up a lady, though her father's gain
Depended still on cattle and on grain,
She followed shifting fashions and aspired
To the high notions baffled pride desired
And all the profits pigs and poultry made
Were gave to Miss for dressing and parade,
To visit balls and plays, fresh hopes to trace,
And try her fortune with a simpering face;
And now and then in London's crowds was shown
To know the world and to the world be known.
All leisure hours while Miss at home sojourned
Passed in preparing till new routs returned,
Or tittle-tattling o'er her shrewd remarks
Of ladies' dresses or attentive sparks:
How Mr So-and-so at such a rout
Fixed his eyes on her all the night about
While the good lady seated by his side
Behind her hand her blushes forced to hide,
Till conscious Miss, in pity she would say
For the poor lady, turned her face away;

And young Squire Dandy just returned from France
How he first chose her from the rest to dance;
And at the play how such a gent resigned
His seat to her and placed himself behind;
How this squire bowed polite at her approach
And Lords e'en nodded as she passed their coach.
Thus Miss in raptures would such things recall
And Pa and Ma in raptures heard it all.
But when an equal would his praise declare
And told young madam that her face was fair,
She might believe the fellow's truth the while
And just in sport might condescend to smile
But frowned his further teasing suit to shun
And deemed it rudeness in a farmer's son.
Thus she went on and visited and dressed
And deemed things earnest that was spoke in jest,
And dreamed at night o'er pride's unchecked desires
Of nodding gentlemen and smiling squires.
To Gretna Green her visions often fled
And rattling coaches lumbered in her head;
Till, hopes grown weary with too long delay,
Caught the green sickness and declined away;
And beauty, like a garment worse for wear,
Fled her pale cheek and left it much too fair.
Then she gave up sick visits, balls and plays,
Where whispers turned to any thing but praise;
All were thrown by like an old-fashioned song
Where she had played show-woman much too long;
And condescended to be kind and plain
And 'mong her equals hoped to find a swain.
Past follies now were hateful to review
And they were hated by her equals too.
Notice from equals vain she tried to court
Or if they noticed 'twas but just in sport.
At last, grown husband-mad, away she ran
Not with Squire Dandy but the servant man.

Young farmer Bigg of this same flimsy class,
Wise among fools and with the wise an ass,

A farming sprout with more than farmer's pride,
Struts like the squire and dresses dignified.
They call him rich, at which his weakness aimed,
But others view him as a fool misnamed.
Yet dress and tattle ladies' hearts can charm
And he's the choice with madams of the farm;
Now with that lady strutting, now with this,
Braced up in stays as slim as sickly Miss,
Shining at Christmas rout and vulgar ball,
The favourite spark and rival of them all.
And oft he'll venture to bemean his pride,
Though bribes and mysteries do their best to hide,
Teasing weak maidens with his pert deceit
Whose lives are humble but whose looks are sweet,
Whose beauty happen to outrival those
With whom the dandy as an equal goes.
Thus maids are ruined oft and mothers made,
As if bewitched, without a father's aid.
Though nods and winks and whispers urge a guess,
Weakness is bribed and hides its heart's distress
To live dishonoured and to die unwed,
For clowns grow jealous when they're once misled.
Thus pointed fingers brand the passing spark
And whispers often guess his deeds are dark;
But friends deny and urge that doubts mislead
And prove the youth above so mean a deed.
The town agrees and leaves his ways at will,
A proud, conceited, meddling fellow still.

Nature in various moods pursues her plan,
And moulds by turns the monkey or the man;
With one she deals out wisdom as a curse
To follow fortune with an empty purse;
The next in opposite extremes is bred:
O'erflowing pockets and an empty head;
Beggars in merit share a squire's estate
And squires untitled meet a beggar's fate.
Fortune's great lottery owns nor rules nor laws;

Fate holds her wealth and reason rarely draws;
Blanks are her lot and merit vainly tries
While heedless folly blunders on the prize.

St Martin's Eve

Now that the year grows wearisome with age
And days grow short and nights excessive long,
No outdoor sports the village hinds engage;
Still is the meadow romp and harvest song
That wont to echo from each merry throng
At dinner hours beneath huge spreading tree.
Rude winds hath done the landscape mickle wrong
That nature in her mirth did ill foresee,
Who clingeth now to hope like shipwrecked folks at sea.

The woods are desolate of song – the sky
Is all forsaken of its joyous crowd;
Martin and swallow there no longer fly
– Huge-seeming rocks and deserts now enshroud
The sky for aye with shadow-shaping cloud.
None there of all those busy tribes remain;
No song is heard save one that wails aloud
From the all lone and melancholy crane
Who like a traveller lost the right road seeks in vain.

The childern hastening in from threatening rain
No longer round the fields for wild fruit run
But at their homes from morn till night remain
And wish in vain to see the welcome sun.
Winter's imprisonment is all begun
Yet when the wind grows troubleous and high,

Pining for freedom like a lovesick nun,
Around the garden's little bounds they fly
Beneath the roaring trees fallen apples to espy.

But spite of all the melancholy moods
That out of doors poor pleasure's heart alarms –
Flood bellowing rivers and wind roaring woods –
The fireside evening owns increasing charms;
What with the tale and eldern wine that warms
In purple bubbles by the blazing fire
Of simple cots and rude old fashioned farms,
They feel as blessed as joys can well desire
And midnight often joins before the guests retire.

And such a group on good St Martin's eve
Was met together upon pleasure bent,
Where tales and fun did cares so well deceive
That the old cottage rung with merriment,
And even the very rafters groaned and bent
Not so much it would seem from tempest's din
That roared without in roaring discontent
As from the merry noise and laugh within,
That seemed as Summer's sports had never absent been.

Beside the fire large apples lay to roast
And in a huge brown pitcher creaming ale
Was warming, seasoned with a nutmeg toast,
The merry group of gossips to regale.
Around her feet the glad cat curled her tail,
Listening the crickets' song with half shut eyes
While in the chimney top loud roared the gale
Its blustering howl of outdoor symphonies
That round the cottage hearth bade happier moods arise.

And circling round the fire the merry folks
Brought up all sports their memory could devise,
Playing upon each other merry jokes;
And now one shuts his hands and archly cries
'Come open wide your mouth and shut your eyes
And see what gifts are sent you' – foolish thing,

He doth as he is bid, and quickly rise
The peals of laughter when they up and fling
The ashes in while he goes spitting from the ring.

And the old dame, though not in laughing luck,
For that same night at one fell sweeping stroke
Mischieving cat that at a mouse had struck
Upon the shelf her best blue china broke;
Yet spite of fate, so funny was the joke
She laughed until her very sides did shake
And some so tittled were they could not smoke,
Laying down their pipes lest they their pipe should break
And laughed and laughed again until their ribs did ache.

Then deftly one with cunning in his eyes
With outstretched hand walks backward in the dark,
Encouraged to the feat with proffered prize
If so he right can touch pretended mark
Made on the wall – and happy as a lark
He chuckles o'er success by hopes prepared,
While one with open mouth like greedy shark
Slives in the place and bites his finger hard;
He bawls for freedom loud and shames his whole reward.

Then came more games of wonderment and fun
Which set poor Hodge's wisdom all aghast,
Who sought three knives to hide them one by one
While one, no conjuror to reveal the past,
Blindfold would tell him where he hid the last.
Hodge hiding two did for the third enquire;
All tittered round and bade him hold it fast
But ah, he shook it from his hands in ire
For while he hid the two they warmed it in the fire.

Then to appease him with his burning hand
They bade him hide himself and they would tell
The very way in which he chose to stand.
Hodge thought the matter most impossible
And on his knees behind the mash-tub fell
And muttering said 'I'll beat 'em now or never',

Crying out 'How stand I?' just to prove the spell;
They answered 'like a fool' and thing so clever
Raised laughter against Hodge more long and loud than ever.

Nor can the aged in such boisterous glee
Escape the tricks for laugh and jest designed:
The old dame takes the bellows on her knee
And puffs in vain, to tricks of roguery blind,
Nor heeds the urchin who lets out the wind
With crafty finger and with cunning skill
That for her life the cause she cannot find,
Until the group, unable to be still,
Laughs out and dame, though tricked, smiles too against her
    will.

Yet mid this strife of joy – on corner stool
One sits all silent, doomed to worst of fate,
Who made one slip in love and played the fool
And since condemned to live without a mate.
No youth again courts once-beguiled Kate,
Though hopes of sweethearts yet perplex her head
And, charms to try by gipsies told of late,
Beneath her pillow lays an onion red
To dream on this same night with whom she is to wed;

And hopes, that like to sunshine warming falls,
Being all the solace to her withering mind,
When they for dancing rise – old, young and all –
She in her corner musing sits behind,
Her pallid cheek upon her hand reclined,
Nursing rude melancholy like a child
Who sighs its silence to the sobbing wind
That in the chimney roars with fury wild
While every other heart to joy is reconciled.

One thumps the warming pan with merry glee
That bright as is a mirror decks the cot;
Another droning as an humble bee
Plays on the muffled comb till piping hot
With over-strained exertion – yet the lot

Is such an happy one that still he plays,
Fatigue and all its countless ills forgot.
All that he wants he wins – for rapture pays
To his unwearied skill right earnest words of praise.

Ah happy hearts, how happy can't be told
To fancy music in such clamorous noise;
Like those converting all they touched to gold
These all they hearken to convert to joys.
Thrice happy hearts – old men as wild as boys
Feel nought of age creep o'er their ecstasies
– Old women whom no cares of life destroys
Dance with the girls – true did the bard surmise
'Where ignorance is bliss 'tis folly to be wise'.

When weary of the dance one reads a tale,
Though puzzled oft to spell a lengthy word:
Stories though often read yet never stale
But gaining interest every time they're heard
With morts of wonderment that ne'er occurred.
Yet simple souls, their faith it knows no stint:
Things least to be believed are most preferred.
All counterfeits, as from truth's sacred mint,
Are readily believed if once put down in print.

Bluebeard and all his murders' dread parade
Are listened to and mourned for and the tear
Drops from the blue eye of the listening maid,
Warm as it fell upon her lover's bier.
None in the circle doubt of what they hear;
It were a sin to doubt o'er tales so true;
So say the old whose wisdom all revere
And unto whom such reverence may be due
For honest good intents, praise that belongs to few.

And Tib a Tinker's daughter is the tale
That doth by wonder their rude hearts engage.
O'er young and old its witchcraft scenes prevail
In the rude legend of her pilgrimage:
How she in servitude did erst engage

To live with an old hag of dreadful fame
Who often fell in freaks of wondrous rage
And played with Tib full many a bitter game
Till e'en the childern round cried out for very shame.

They read how once, to thrash her into chaff,
The fearful witch tied Tibby in a sack
And hied her to the wood to seek a staff
That might be strong enough her bones to whack,
But lucky Tib escaped ere she came back
And tied up dog and cat her doom to share
And pots and pans – and loud the howl and crack
That rose when the old witch with inky hair
Began the sack to thrash with no intent to spare;

And when she found her unrevenged mistake
Her rage more fearful grew, but all in vain
For fear no more caused Tibby's heart to ache.
She far away from the old hag's domain
Ran heartsomely a better place to gain.
And here the younkers' tongues grew wonder glib
With gladness, and the reader stopped again,
Declaring all too true to be a fib
And urged full glasses round to drink success to Tib.

And when her sorrows and her pilgrimage –
The plot of most new novels and old tales –
Grew to a close, her beauty did presage
Luck in the wind – and fortune spread her sails
In favouring bounty to Tib's Summer gales.
All praised her beauty and the lucky day
At length its rosy smiling face unveils
When Tib of course became a lady gay,
And loud the listeners laughed while childern turned to play.

Anon the clock counts twelve and 'mid their joys
The startled blackbird smoothes its feathers down
That in its cage grew weary of their noise
– The merry maiden and the noisy clown
Prepare for home and down the straggling town

To seek their cottages they tittering go;
Heartened with sports and stout ale berry-brown,
Beside their dames like Chanticleer they crow
While every lanthorn flings long gleams along the snow.

Birds and Beasts

The Wren

Why is the cuckoo's melody preferred
And nightingale's rich song so fondly praised
In poets' rhymes? Is there no other bird
Of nature's minstrelsy that oft hath raised
One's heart to ecstasy and mirth as well?
I judge not how another's taste is caught;
With mine there's other birds that bear the bell
Whose song hath crowds of happy memories brought.
Such the wood Robin singing in the dell
And little Wren that many a time hath sought
Shelter from showers in huts where I did dwell
In early Spring, the tenant of the plain,
Tenting my sheep, and still they come to tell
The happy stories of the past again.

Sonnet: The Crow

How peaceable it seems for lonely men
To see a crow fly in the thin blue sky
Over the woods and fields, o'er level fen.
It speaks of villages, or cottage nigh
Behind the neighbouring woods – when March winds high
Tear off the branches of the huge old oak.
I love to see these chimney-sweeps sail by
And hear them o'er the gnarled forest croak,
Then sosh askew from the hid woodman's stroke
That in the woods their daily labours ply.
I love the sooty crow, nor would provoke

Its March day exercise of croaking joy;
I love to see it sailing to and fro
While fields, and woods and waters spread below.

Sonnet: 'I love to hear the evening crows go by'

I love to hear the evening crows go by
And see the starnels darken down the sky.
The bleaching stack the bustling sparrow leaves
And plops with merry note beneath the eaves.
The odd and lated pigeon bounces by
As if a wary watching hawk was nigh,
While far and fearing nothing, high and slow,
The stranger birds to distant places go,
While short of flight the evening robin comes
To watch the maiden sweeping out the crumbs
Nor fears the idle shout of passing boy
But pecks about the door and sings for joy;
Then in the hovel where the cows are fed
Finds till the morning comes a pleasant bed.

The Skylark

The rolls and harrows lie at rest beside
The battered road and, spreading far and wide
Above the russet clods, the corn is seen
Sprouting its spiry points of tender green,
Where squats the hare to terrors wide awake
Like some brown clod the harrows failed to break,
While neath the warm hedge boys stray far from home

To crop the early blossoms as they come;
Where buttercups will make them eager run
Opening their golden caskets to the sun
To see who shall be first to pluck the prize;
And from their hurry up the skylark flies
And o'er her half-formed nest with happy wings
Winnows the air – till in the clouds she sings,
Then hangs a dust spot in the sunny skies
And drops and drops till in her nest she lies
Where boys unheeding passed – ne'er dreaming then
That birds which flew so high – would drop again
To nests upon the ground where any thing
May come at to destroy. Had they the wing
Like such a bird, themselves would be too proud
And build on nothing but a passing cloud,
As free from danger as the heavens are free
From pain and toil – there would they build and be
And sail about the world to scenes unheard
Of and unseen – O were they but a bird.
So think they while they listen to its song
And smile and fancy and so pass along
While its low nest moist with the dews of morn
Lie safely with the leveret in the corn.

Sonnet: 'Among the orchard weeds'

Among the orchard weeds, from every search
Snugly and sure, the old hen's nest is made,
Who cackles every morning from her perch
To tell the servant girl new eggs are laid,
Who lays her washing by and far and near
Goes seeking all about from day to day
And, stung with nettles, tramples everywhere,
But still the cackling pullet lays away.
The boy on Sundays goes the stack to pull
In hopes to find her there but nought is seen

And takes his hat and thinks to find it full
She's laid so long, so many might have been;
But nought is found and all is given o'er
Till the young brood come chirping to the door.

The Landrail

How sweet and pleasant grows the way
Through Summer time again
While landrails call from day to day
Amid the grass and grain.

We hear it in the weeding time
When knee deep waves the corn,
We hear it in the Summer's prime
Through meadows night and morn;

And now I hear it in the grass
That grows as sweet again,
And let a minute's notice pass
And now 'tis in the grain.

'Tis like a fancy everywhere,
A sort of living doubt;
We know 'tis something but it ne'er
Will blab the secret out.

If heard in close or meadow plots
It flies if we pursue,
But follows if we notice not
The close and meadow through.

Boys know the note of many a bird
In their birdnesting rounds
But when the landrail's noise is heard
They wonder at the sounds.

They look in every tuft of grass
That's in their rambles met;
They peep in every bush they pass
And none the wiser get.

And still they hear the craiking sound
And still they wonder why:
It surely can't be under ground
Nor is it in the sky.

And yet 'tis heard in every vale,
An undiscovered song,
And makes a pleasant wonder tale
For all the summer long.

The shepherd whistles through his hands
And starts with many a whoop
His busy dog across the lands
In hopes to fright it up.

'Tis still a minute's length or more
Till dogs are off and gone,
Then sings and louder than before
But keeps the secret on.

Yet accident will often meet
The nest within its way
And weeders when they weed the wheat
Discover where they lay.

And mowers on the meadow lea
Chance on their noisy guest
And wonder what the bird can be
That lays without a nest.

In simple holes that birds will rake
When dusting in the ground
They drop their eggs of curious make,
Deep blotched and nearly round,

A mystery still to men and boys
Who know not where they lay
And guess it but a summer noise
Among the meadow hay.

Sonnet: The Nightingale

This is the month the Nightingale, clod-brown,
   Is heard among the woodland shady boughs;
This is the time when in the vale, grass-grown,
   The maiden hears at eve her lover's vows
   What time the blue mist round her patient cows
Dim rises from the grass and half conceals
   Their dappled hides – I hear the Nightingale,
That from the little blackthorn spinny steals
   To the old hazel hedge that skirts the vale,
And, still unseen, sings sweet – the ploughman feels
   The thrilling music as he goes along
And imitates and listens – while the fields
   Lose all their paths in dusk to lead him wrong
   Still sings the Nightingale her sweet melodious song.

The Nightingale's Nest

Up this green woodland ride let's softly rove
And list the nightingale – she dwelleth here.
Hush! let the wood gate softly clap – for fear
The noise might drive her from her home of love;
For here I've heard her many a merry year
At morn and eve, nay, all the live-long day
As though she lived on song – this very spot,

Just where that old man's beard all wildly trails
Rude arbours o'er the road and stops the way,
And where that child its bluebell flowers hath got
Laughing and creeping through the mossy rails.
There have I hunted like a very boy
Creeping on hands and knees through matted thorns
To find her nest and see her feed her young,
And vainly did I many hours employ:
All seemed as hidden as a thought unborn.
And where these crimping fern leaves ramp among
The hazel's underboughs – I've nestled down
And watched her while she sung – and her renown
Hath made me marvel that so famed a bird
Should have no better dress than russet brown.
Her wings would tremble in her ecstasy
And feathers stand on end as 'twere with joy
And mouth wide open to release her heart
Of its out-sobbing songs – the happiest part
Of Summer's fame she shared – for so to me
Did happy fancies shapen her employ;
But if I touched a bush or scarcely stirred
All in a moment stopped – I watched in vain:
The timid bird had left the hazel bush
And at a distance hid to sing again,
Lost in a wilderness of listening leaves.
Rich ecstasy would pour its luscious strain
Till envy spurred the emulating thrush
To start less wild and scarce inferior songs,
For cares with him for half the year remain
To damp the ardour of his speckled breast,
While nightingales to Summer's life belongs,
And naked trees and Winter's nipping wrongs
Are strangers to her music and her rest.
Her joys are evergreen; her world is wide.
– Hark! there she is, as usual, let's be hush,
For in this blackthorn clump if rightly guessed
Her curious house is hidden – part aside
These hazel branches in a gentle way
And stoop right cautious 'neath the rustling boughs,
For we will have another search today

And hunt this fern-strown thorn-clump round and round,
And where this seeded woodgrass idly bows
We'll wade right through; it is a likely nook.
In such-like spots and often on the ground
They'll build where rude boys never think to look.
Aye, as I live, her secret nest is here,
Upon this whitethorn stulp – I've searched about
For hours in vain – there; put that bramble by.
Nay, trample on its branches and get near
– How subtle is the bird; she started out
And raised a plaintive note of danger nigh
Ere we were past the brambles, and now near
Her nest she sudden stops – as choking fear
That might betray her home – so even now
We'll leave it as we found it – safety's guard
Of pathless solitudes shall keep it still.
See; there she's sitting on the old oak bough,
Mute in her fears – our presence doth retard
Her joys and doubt turns every rapture chill.
    Sing on, sweet bird; may no worse hap befall
Thy visions than the fear that now deceives.
We will not plunder music of its dower
Nor turn this spot of happiness to thrall,
For melody seems hid in every flower
That blossoms near thy home – these harebells all
Seems bowing with the beautiful in song,
And gaping cuckoo with its spotted leaves
Seems blushing of the singing it has heard.
How curious is the nest. No other bird
Uses such loose materials or weaves
Their dwellings in such spots – dead oaken leaves
Are placed without and velvet moss within
And little scraps of grass – and scant and spare
Of what seems scarce materials, down and hair,
For from man's haunts she seemeth nought to win.
Yet nature is the builder and contrives
Homes for her childern's comfort even here
Where solitude's disciples spend their lives
Unseen save when a wanderer passes near
That loves such pleasant places – Deep adown

The nest is made an hermit's mossy cell.
Snug lies her curious eggs, in number five,
Of deadened green or rather olive brown
And the old prickly thorn bush guards them well.
And here we'll leave them still unknown to wrong
As the old woodland's legacy of song.

The Yellowhammer's Nest

Just by the wooden brig a bird flew up,
Frit by the cow-boy as he scrambled down
To reach the misty dewberry – let us stoop
And seek its nest – the brook we need not dread;
'Tis scarcely deep enough a bee to drown,
So it sings harmless o'er its pebbly bed
– Aye, here it is, stuck close beside the bank
Beneath the bunch of grass that spindles rank
Its husk seeds tall and high – 'tis rudely planned
Of bleached stubbles and the withered fare
That last year's harvest left upon the land,
Lined thinly with the horse's sable hair
– Five eggs pen-scribbled over lilac shells
Resembling writing scrawls, which fancy reads
As nature's poesy and pastoral spells;
They are the yellowhammer's and she dwells
A poet-like – where brooks and flowery weeds
As sweet as Castaly to fancy seems
And that old molehill like as Parnass hill
On which her partner haply sits and dreams
O'er all his joy of song – so leave it still,
A happy home of sunshine, flowers and streams.
Yet in the sweetest places cometh ill,

A noisome weed that burthens every soil,
For snakes are known with chill and deadly coil
To watch such nests and seize the helpless young
And like as though the plague became a guest,
Leaving a houseless home a ruined nest
And mournful hath the little warblers sung
When such like woes hath rent its little breast.

The Pettichap's Nest

Well, in my many walks I rarely found
A place less likely for a bird to form
Its nest, close by the rut-gulled waggon road
And on the almost bare foot-trodden ground,
With scarce a clump of grass to keep it warm
And not a thistle spreads its spears abroad
Or prickly bush to shield it from harm's way,
And yet so snugly made that none may spy
It out save accident – and you and I
Had surely passed it on our walk today
Had chance not led us by it – nay e'en now
Had not the old bird heard us trampling by
And fluttered out – we had not seen it lie
Brown as the roadway side – small bits of hay
Plucked from the old propped-haystack's pleachy brow
And withered leaves make up its outward walls
That from the snub-oak dotterel yearly falls
And in the old hedge bottom rot away.
Built like an oven with a little hole
Hard to discover – that snug entrance wins,
Scarcely admitting e'en two fingers in
And lined with feathers warm as silken stole
And soft as seats of down for painless ease

And full of eggs scarce bigger e'en than peas.
Here's one most delicate, with spots as small
As dust – and of a faint and pinky red
– We'll let them be and safety guard them well,
For fear's rude paths around are thickly spread
And they are left to many dangers' ways
When green grasshopper's jump might break the shells,
While lowing oxen pass them morn and night
And restless sheep around them hourly stray
And no grass springs but hungry horses bite
That trample past them twenty times a day.
Yet like a miracle in safety's lap
They still abide unhurt and out of sight
– Stop; here's the bird. That woodman at the gap
Hath put it from the hedge – 'tis olive green.
Well I declare, it is the pettichaps;
Not bigger than the wren and seldom seen.
I've often found their nests in chance's way
When I in pathless woods did idly roam
But never did I dream until today
A spot like this would be her chosen home.

Sonnets: The Hedgehog

The hedgehog hides beneath the rotten hedge
And makes a great round nest of grass and sedge,
Or in a bush or in a hollow tree,
And many often stoops and say they see
Him roll and fill his prickles full of crabs
And creep away and, where the magpie dabs
His wing at muddy dyke in aged root,
He makes a nest and fills it full of fruit;
On the hedge-bottom hunts for crabs and sloes

And whistles like a cricket as he goes.
It rolls up like a ball, a shapeless hog,
When gipsies hunt it with their noisy dogs.
I've seen it in their camps; they call it sweet,
Though black and bitter and unsavoury meat.

But they who hunt the fields for rotten meat
And wash in muddy dyke and call it sweet
And eat what dogs refuse where'er they dwell,
Care little either for the taste or smell.
They say they milk the cows and when they lie
Nibble their fleshy teats and make them dry;
But they who've seen the small head like a hog,
Rolled up to meet the savage of a dog
With mouth scarce big enough to hold a straw,
Will ne'er believe what no one ever saw.
But still they hunt the hedges all about
And shepherd dogs are trained to hunt them out.
They hurl with savage force the stick and stone
And no one cares and still the strife goes on.

Sonnet: 'One day when all the woods were bare'

One day when all the woods were bare and blea
I wandered out to take a pleasant walk
And saw a strange-formed nest on stoven tree
Where startled pigeon buzzed from bouncing hawk.
I wondered strangely what the nest could be
And thought besure it was some foreign bird;
So up I scrambled in the highest glee
And my heart jumped at every thing that stirred.

'Twas oval-shaped; strange wonder filled my breast.
I hoped to catch the old one on the nest,
When something bolted out. I turned to see
And a brown squirrel pattered up the tree.
'Twas lined with moss and leaves, compact and strong.
I sluthered down and wondering went along.

Sonnet: 'I found a ball of grass among the hay'

I found a ball of grass among the hay
And progged it as I passed and went away,
And when I looked I fancied something stirred
And turned again and hoped to catch the bird,
When out an old mouse bolted in the wheat
With all her young ones hanging at her teats.
She looked so odd and so grotesque to me,
I ran and wondered what the thing could be
And pushed the knapweed bunches where I stood,
When the mouse hurried from the crawling brood.
The young ones squeaked and when I went away
She found her nest again among the hay.
The water o'er the pebbles scarce could run
And broad old cesspools glittered in the sun.

The Ants

What wonder strikes the curious while he views
The black ants' city by a rotten tree
Or woodland bank – in ignorance we muse,
Pausing amazed, we know not what we see –
Such government and order there to be;
Some looking on and urging some to toil,
Dragging their loads of bent stalks slavishly
And what's more wonderful – big loads that foil
One ant or two to carry quickly, then
A swarm flocks round to help their fellow men.
Surely they speak a language whisperingly
Too fine for us to hear, and sure their ways
Prove they have kings and laws and them to be
Deformed remnants of the fairy days.

Little Trotty Wagtail

Little trotty wagtail, he went in the rain
And, tittering tottering sideways, he ne'er got straight again.
He stooped to get a worm and looked up to catch a fly
And then he flew away ere his feathers they were dry.

Little trotty wagtail, he waddled in the mud
And left his little foot-marks, trample where he would.
He waddled in the water pudge and waggle went his tail
And chirruped up his wings to dry upon the garden rail.

Little trotty wagtail, you nimble all about
And in the dimpling water pudge you waddle in and out.
Your home is nigh at hand and in the warm pigsty,
So little Master Wagtail, I'll bid you a 'Goodbye'.

Love

Song: 'The morning mist is changing blue'

The morning mist is changing blue
Like smoke among the bushes;
The one arched brig shines clearly through
Near beds of water-rushes;
The cows lie in the pasture fair,
And maids the hay was turning
When a maid went by with inky hair
As bonny as the morning.

Her face was smiling like the sun,
Her bosom swelled; a treasure
She looked – my heart was fairly won;
I felt both pain and pleasure.
But pain I know can soon be well;
Old friendships are sincerest,
And for my life I cannot tell
Which feeling was the dearest.

How bright the day, how clear the sky,
How sweet the woods were waving;
The river ran as gently by,
The waterfall was raving;
All nature in her sweetest dress
Was still but sweetly dawning
That day the happiest maid went by
As bonny as the morning.

First Love's Recollections

First love will with the heart remain
When all its hopes are by,
As frail rose blossoms still retain
Their fragrance till they die;
And joy's first dreams will haunt the mind
With shades from whence they sprung,
As Summer leaves the stems behind
On which Spring's blossoms hung.

Mary, I dare not call thee dear,
I've lost that right so long,
Yet once again I vex thine ear
With memory's idle song.
Had time and change not blotted out
The love of former days
Thou wert the last that I should doubt
Of pleasing with my praise.

When honied tokens from each tongue
Told with what truth we loved,
How rapturous to thy lips I clung
Whilst nought but smiles reproved;
But now methinks if one kind word
Were whispered in thine ear
Thou'dst startle like an untamed bird
And blush with wilder fear.

How loath to part, how fond to meet
Had we two used to be;
At sunset with what eager feet
I hastened on to thee.
Scarce nine days passed ere we met
In Spring, nay wintry weather;
Now nine years' suns have risen and set
Nor found us once together.

Thy face was so familiar grown,
Thyself so often by,
A moment's memory when alone
Would bring thee to mine eye;
But now my very dreams forget
That witching look to trace;
Though there thy beauty lingers yet,
It wears a stranger face.

I felt a pride to name thy name
But now that pride hath flown,
My words e'en seem to blush for shame
That own I love thee on.
I felt I then thy heart did share
Nor urged a binding vow;
But much I doubt if thou couldst spare
One word of kindness now.

And what is now my name to thee,
Though once nought seemed so dear?
Perhaps a jest in hours of glee
To please some idle ear;
And yet like counterfeits with me
Impressions linger on
Though all the gilded finery
That passed for truth is gone.

Ere the world smiled upon my lays,
A sweeter meed was mine –
Thy blushing look of ready praise
Was raised at every line,
But now methinks thy fervent love
Is changed to scorn severe
And songs that other hearts approve
Seem discord to thine ear.

When last thy gentle cheek I pressed
And heard thee feign adieu,

I little thought that seeming jest
Would prove a word so true.
A fate like this hath oft befell
E'en loftier hopes than ours;
Spring bids full many buds to swell
That ne'er can grow to flowers.

Ballad: 'I dreamt not what it was to woo'

I dreamt not what it was to woo
And felt my heart secure
Till Robin dropped a word or two
Last evening on the moor.
Though with no flattering words the while
His suit he urged to move,
Fond ways informed me with a smile
How sweet it was to love.

He left the path to let me pass,
The dropping dews to shun,
And walked himself among the grass;
I deemed it kindly done;
And when his hand was held to me
As o'er each stile we went,
I deemed it rude to say him nay
And manners to consent.

He saw me to the town and then
He sighed but kissed me not,
And whispered 'We shall meet again'
But didn't say for what;
Yet on my breast his cheek had lain
And, though it gently pressed,
It bruised my heart and left a pain
That robs it of its rest.

Song: 'Say what is love'

Say what is love – to live in vain;
To live and die and live again.

Say what is love – is it to be
In prison still and still be free

Or seem as free – alone and prove
The hopeless hopes of real love?

Does real love on earth exist?
'Tis like a sunbeam on the mist

That fades and nowhere will remain
And nowhere is o'ertook again.

Say what is love – a blooming name,
A rose leaf on the page of fame

That blooms, then fades – to cheat no more
And is what nothing was before.

Say what is love – whate'er it be,
It centres Mary still with thee.

Song: 'Love lives beyond'

Love lives beyond
The tomb – the earth – which fades like dew.
I love the fond,
The faithful and the true.

Love lives in sleep;
The happiness of healthy dreams

Eve's dews may weep
But love delightful seems.

'Tis seen in flowers
And in the even's pearly dew,
On earth's green hours
And in the heaven's eternal blue.

'Tis heard in Spring
When light and sunbeams warm and kind
On angel's wing
Bring love and music to the mind;

And where is voice
So young and beautifully sweet
As nature's choice
When Spring and lovers meet?

Love lives beyond
The tomb, the earth, the flowers and dew;
I love the fond,
The faithful, young and true.

Ballad: 'The Spring returns, the pewit screams'

The Spring returns, the pewit screams
Loud welcomes to the dawning;
Though harsh and ill as now it seems,
'Twas music last May morning.
The grass so green – the daisy gay
Wakes no joy in my bosom,
Although the garland last Mayday
Wore not a finer blossom.

For by this bridge my Mary sat
And praised the screaming plover
As first to hail the day – when I
Confessed myself her lover;
And at that moment stooping down
I plucked a daisy blossom
Which smilingly she called her own
May-garland for her bosom.

And in her breast she hid it there
As true love's happy omen;
Gold had not claimed a safer care.
I thought love's name was woman.
I claimed a kiss she laughed away,
I sweetly sold the blossom;
I thought myself a king that day;
My throne was beauty's bosom,

And little thought an evil hour
Was bringing clouds around me
And least of all that little flower
Would turn a thorn to wound me;
She showed me after many days,
Though withered, how she prized it,
And then she leaned to wealthy praise
And my poor love – despised it.

Aloud the whirring pewit screams,
The daisy blooms as gaily,
But where is Mary? – absence seems
To ask that question daily.
Nowhere on earth where joy can be
To glad me with her pleasure;
Another name she owns – to me
She is as stolen treasure.

When lovers part, the longest mile
Leaves hope of some returning;
Though mine's close by, no hope the while
Within my heart is burning.

One hour would bring me to her door
Yet, sad and lonely-hearted,
If seas between us both should roar
We were not further parted.

Though I could reach her with my hand
Ere sun the earth goes under,
Her heart from mine – the sea and land
Are not more far asunder.
The wind and clouds, now here, now there,
Hold not such strange dominion
As woman's cold perverted will
And soon-estranged opinion.

An Invite to Eternity

Wilt thou go with me sweet maid?
Say, maiden, wilt thou go with me
Through the valley depths of shade,
Of night and dark obscurity,
Where the path hath lost its way,
Where the sun forgets the day,
Where there's nor life nor light to see?
Sweet maiden, wilt thou go with me?

Where stones will turn to flooding streams,
Where plains will rise like ocean waves,
Where life will fade like visioned dreams
And mountains darken into caves,
Say, maiden, wilt thou go with me
Through this sad non-identity,
Where parents live and are forgot
And sisters live and know us not?

Say, maiden, wilt thou go with me
In this strange death of life to be,

To live in death and be the same
Without this life, or home, or name;
At once to be, and not to be,
That was, and is not – yet to see
Things pass like shadows – and the sky
Above, below, around us lie?

The land of shadows wilt thou trace
And look – nor know each other's face;
The present mixed with reasons gone
And past, and present all as one.
Say, maiden, can thy life be led
To join the living with the dead?
Then trace thy footsteps on with me;
We're wed to one eternity.

Love and Memory

Thou art gone the dark journey
That leaves no returning.
'Tis fruitless to mourn thee
But who can help mourning,
To think of the life
That did laugh on thy brow
In the beautiful past,
Left so desolate now,

When youth seemed immortal
So sweet did it weave
Heaven's halo around thee
Earth's hopes to deceive?
Thou fairest and dearest,
Where many were fair,
To my heart thou art nearest
Though this name is but there.

The nearer the fountain,
More pure the stream flows,
And sweeter to fancy
The bud of the rose;
And now thou'rt in heaven
More pure is the birth
Of thoughts that wake of thee
Than ought upon earth.

As a bud green in Spring,
As a rose blown in June,
Thy beauty looked out
And departed as soon.
Heaven saw thee too fair
For earth's tenants of clay
And ere age did thee wrong
Thou wert summoned away.

I know thou art happy;
Why in grief need I be?
Yet I am and the more so
To feel it's for thee,
For thy presence possessed,
As thy absence destroyed,
The most that I loved
And the all I enjoyed.

So I try to seek pleasure
But vainly I try,
Now joy's cup is drained
And hope's fountain is dry.
I mix with the living
Yet what do I see?
Only more cause for sorrow
In losing of thee.

The year has its Winter
As well as its May,
So the sweetest must leave us
And the fairest decay.

Suns leave us to night
And their light none may borrow,
So joy retreats from us
Overtaken by sorrow.

The sun greets the Spring
And the blossom the bee,
The grass the blea hill
And the leaf the bare tree;
But suns nor yet seasons
As sweet as they be
Shall ever more greet me
With tidings of thee.

The voice of the cuckoo
Is merry at noon
And the song of the nightingale
Gladdens the moon,
But the gayest today
May be saddest tomorrow
And the loudest in joy
Sink the deepest in sorrow.

For the lovely in death
And the fairest must die,
Fall once and for ever
Like stars from the sky;
So in vain do I mourn thee;
I know it's in vain –
Who would wish thee from joy
To earth's troubles again?

Yet thy love shed upon me
Life more than mine own,
And now thou art from me
My being is gone.
Words know not my grief
Thus without thee to dwell,
Yet in one I felt all
When life bade thee farewell.

Loss and the Politics of Nature

Remembrances

Summer pleasures they are gone, like to visions every one,
And the cloudy days of Autumn and of Winter cometh on.
I tried to call them back but unbidden they are gone
Far away from heart and eye and for ever far away.
Dear heart and can it be that such raptures meet decay?
I thought them all eternal when by Langley Bush I lay;
I thought them joys eternal when I used to shout and play
On its bank at 'clink and bandy', 'chock' and 'taw' and ducking
    stone,
Where silence sitteth now on the wild heath as her own
Like a ruin of the past all alone.

When I used to lie and sing by old Eastwell's boiling spring,
When I used to tie the willow boughs together for a 'swing',
And fish with crooked pins and thread and never catch a thing
With heart just like a feather – now as heavy as a stone –
When beneath old Lea Close Oak I the bottom branches broke
To make our harvest cart like so many working folk;
And then to cut a straw at the brook to have a soak.
O I never dreamed of parting or that trouble had a sting,
Or that pleasures like a flock of birds would ever take to wing
Leaving nothing but a little naked spring.

When jumping time away on old Crossberry Way
And eating haws like sugar plums ere they had lost the May
And skipping like a leveret before the peep of day
On the roly poly up and downs of pleasant Swordy Well,
When in Round Oak's narrow lane as the south got black again
We sought the hollow ash that was shelter from the rain
With our pockets full of peas we had stolen from the grain;
How delicious was the dinner time on such a showery day.

O words are poor receipts for what time hath stole away –
The ancient pulpit trees and the play.

When for school o'er 'little field' with its brook and wooden brig
Where I swaggered like a man though I was not half so big,
While I held my little plough though 'twas but a willow twig
And drove my team along made of nothing but a name:
'Gee hep' and 'hoit' and 'woi' – O, I never call to mind
These pleasant names of places but I leave a sigh behind
When I see the little mouldiwarps hang sweeing to the wind
On the only aged willow that in all the field remains;
And nature hides her face where they're sweeing in their chains
And in a silent murmuring complains.

Here was commons for their hills where they seek for freedom
    still,
Though every common's gone and though traps are set to kill
The little homeless miners – O it turns my bosom chill
When I think of old Sneap Green, Puddocks Nook and Hilly Snow
Where bramble bushes grew and the daisy gemmed in dew
And the hills of silken grass like to cushions to the view,
Where we threw the pismire crumbs when we'd nothing else to
    do.
All levelled like a desert by the never-weary plough,
All vanished like the sun where that cloud is passing now
And settled here for ever on its brow.

O I never thought that joys would run away from boys
Or that boys would change their minds and forsake such Summer
    joys,
But alack, I never dreamed that the world had other toys
To petrify first feelings like the fable into stone,
Till I found the pleasure past and a Winter come at last.
Then the fields were sudden bare and the sky got overcast
And boyhood's pleasing haunts like a blossom in the blast
Was shrivelled to a withered weed and trampled down and done,
Till vanished was the morning Spring and set that Summer sun
And Winter fought her battle-strife and won.

By Langley Bush I roam but the bush hath left its hill;
On Cowper Green I stray – 'tis a desert strange and chill –

And spreading Lea Close Oak ere decay had penned its will
To the axe of the spoiler and self interest fell a prey;
And Crossberry Way and old Round Oak's narrow lane
With its hollow trees like pulpits I shall never see again.
Enclosure like a Bonaparte let not a thing remain,
It levelled every bush and tree and levelled every hill
And hung the moles for traitors – though the brook is running still,
It runs a naked brook, cold and chill.

O had I known as then joy had left the paths of men,
I had watched her night and day, be sure, and never slept again;
And when she turned to go, O I'd caught her mantle then
And wooed her like a lover by my lonely side to stay,
Aye, knelt and worshipped on, as love in beauty's bower,
And clung upon her smiles as a bee upon a flower
And gave her heart my poesies all cropt in a sunny hour
As keepsakes and pledges all to never fade away;
But love never heeded to treasure up the May
So it went the common road with decay.

The Flitting

I've left mine own old home of homes,
Green fields and every pleasant place;
The Summer like a stranger comes;
I pause and hardly know her face.
I miss the hazel's happy green,
The bluebell's quiet hanging blooms
Where envy's sneer was never seen,
Where staring malice never comes.

I miss the heath, its yellow furze,
Molehills and rabbit tracks that lead
Through besom ling and teazle burrs

That spread a wilderness indeed;
The woodland oaks and all below
That their white powdered branches shield,
The mossy paths – the very crow
Croaks music in my native field.

I sit me in my corner chair
That seems to feel itself from home
And hear bird-music here and there
From hawthorn hedge and orchard come;
I hear, but all is strange and new
– I sat on my old bench in June.
The sailing puddock's shrill 'peelew'
O'er Royce Wood seemed a sweeter tune.

I walk adown the narrow lane;
The nightingale is singing now
But like to me she seems at loss
For Royce Wood and its shielding bough.
I lean upon the window sill;
The trees and Summer happy seem;
Green, sunny green, they shine – but still
My heart goes far away to dream

Of happiness, and thoughts arise
With home-bred pictures many a one,
Green lanes that shut out burning skies
And old crooked stiles to rest upon.
Above them hangs the maple tree,
Below grass swells a velvet hill,
And little footpaths sweet to see
Goes seeking sweeter places still,

With by and by a brook to cross
O'er which a little arch is thrown.
No brook is here; I feel the loss,
From home and friends and all alone.

The stone pit with its shelvy sides
Seemed hanging rocks in my esteem.
I miss the prospect far and wide
From Langley Bush and so I seem

Alone and in a stranger scene,
Far, far from spots my heart esteems,
The closen with their ancient green,
Heaths, woods and pastures, sunny streams.
The hawthorns here were hung with May
But still they seem in deader green;
The sun e'en seems to lose its way
Nor knows the quarter it is in.

I dwell on trifles like a child,
I feel as ill becomes a man
And still my thoughts like weedlings wild
Grow up to blossom where they can;
They turn to places known so long
And feel that joy was dwelling there,
So home-fed pleasures fill the song
That has no present joys to heir.

I read in books for happiness
But books are like the sea to joy:
They change – as well give age the glass
To hunt its visage when a boy.
For books they follow fashions new
And throw all old esteems away.
In crowded streets flowers never grew
But many there hath died away.

Some sing the pomps of chivalry
As legends of the ancient time
Where gold and pearls and mystery
Are shadows painted for sublime,
But passions of sublimity

Belong to plain and simpler things
And David underneath a tree
Sought, when a shepherd, Salem's springs

Where moss did into cushions spring
Forming a seat of velvet hue,
A small unnoticed trifling thing
To all but heaven's hailing dew.
And David's crown hath passed away
Yet poesy breathes his shepherd skill;
His palace lost – and to this day
The little moss is blooming still.

Strange scenes mere shadows are to me,
Vague unpersonifying things.
I love with my old home to be
By quiet woods and gravel springs
Where little pebbles wear as smooth
As hermits' beads by gentle floods,
Whose noises doth my spirits soothe
And warms them into singing moods.

Here every tree is strange to me,
All foreign things where'er I go;
There's none where boyhood made a swee
Or clambered up to rob a crow;
No hollow tree or woodland bower
Well-known when joy was beating high,
Where beauty ran to shun a shower
And love took pains to keep her dry,

And laid the shoaf upon the ground
To keep her from the dripping grass
And ran for stowks and set them round
Till scarce a drop of rain could pass
Through – where the maidens they reclined
And sung sweet ballads, now forgot,

Which brought sweet memories to the mind;
But here no memory knows them not.

There have I sat by many a tree
And leaned o'er many a rural stile
And conned my thoughts as joys to me,
Nought heeding who might frown or smile.
'Twas nature's beauty that inspired
My heart with raptures not its own,
And she's a fame that never tires;
How could I feel myself alone?

No – pasture molehills used to lie
And talk to me of sunny days,
And then the glad sheep resting by
All still in ruminating praise
Of Summer and the pleasant place,
And every weed and blossom too
Was looking upward in my face
With friendship's welcome 'How do ye do':

All tenants of an ancient place
And heirs of noble heritage,
Coeval they with Adam's race
And blest with more substantial age;
For when the world first saw the sun
These little flowers beheld him too,
And when his love for earth begun
They were the first his smiles to woo.

There little lambtoe bunches springs
In red-tinged and begolden dye
For ever, and like China kings
They come, but never seem to die.
There May-blooms with its little threads
Still comes upon the thorny bowers

And ne'er forgets those pinky threads
Like fairy pins amid the flowers.

And still they bloom as on the day
They first crowned wilderness and rock,
When Abel haply crowned with May
The firstlings of his little flock;
And Eve might from the matted thorn
To deck her lone and lovely brow
Reach that same rose that heedless scorn
Misnames as the dog rosey now.

Give me no highflown fangled things,
No haughty pomp in marching chime
Where muses play on golden strings
And splendour passes for sublime,
Where cities stretch as far as fame
And fancy's straining eye can go,
And piled until the sky for shame
Is stooping far away below.

I love the verse that mild and bland
Breathes of green fields and open sky;
I love the muse that in her hand
Bears wreaths of native poesy,
Who walks, nor skips the pasture brook
In scorn – but by the drinking horse
Leans o'er its little brig to look
How far the sallows lean across,

And feels a rapture in her breast
Upon their root-fringed grains to mark
A hermit moorhen's sedgy nest
Just like a naiad's Summer bark.
She counts the eggs she cannot reach,
Admires the spot and loves it well
And yearns, so nature's lessons teach,
Amid such neighbourhoods to dwell.

I love the muse who sits her down
Upon the molehill's little lap,
Who feels no fear to stain her gown
And pauses by the hedgerow gap
Not with that affectation, praise
Of song to sing, and never see
A field flower grow in all her days
Or e'en a forest's aged tree.

E'en here my simple feelings nurse
A love for every simple weed,
And e'en this little 'shepherd's purse'
Grieves me to cut it up – Indeed
I feel at times a love and joy
For every weed and every thing,
A feeling kindred from a boy,
A feeling brought with every Spring.

And why? – this 'shepherd's purse' that grows
In this strange spot, in days gone by
Grew in the little garden rows
Of my old home now left – And I
Feel what I never felt before:
This weed an ancient neighbour here,
And though I own the spot no more,
Its every trifle makes it dear.

The Ivy at the parlour end,
The woodbine at the garden gate
Are all and each affection's friend
That rendered parting desolate;
But times will change and friends must part
And nature still can make amends.
Their memory lingers round the heart
Like life, whose essence is its friends.

Time looks on pomp with careless moods
Or killing apathy's disdain;

– So where old marble cities stood
Poor persecuted weeds remain.
She feels a love for little things
That very few can feel beside,
And still the grass eternal springs
Where castles stood and grandeur died.

Decay, a Ballad

O poesy is on the wane,
For fancy's visions all unfitting;
I hardly know her face again;
Nature herself seems on the flitting.
The fields grow old and common things –
The grass, the sky, the winds a-blowing,
And spots where still a beauty clings –
Are sighing 'Going, all a-going'.
O, poesy is on the wane;
I hardly know her face again.

The bank with brambles overspread
And little molehills round about it
Was more to me than laurel shades
With paths and gravel finely clouted,
And streaking here and streaking there
Through shaven grass and many a border
With rutty lanes had no compare
And heaths were in a richer order;
But poesy is in its wane;
I hardly know her face again.

I sat with love by pasture streams;
Aye, beauty's self was sitting by
Till fields did more than Edens seem
Nor could I tell the reason why.

I often drank when not a-dry
To pledge her health in draughts divine;
Smiles made it nectar from the sky,
Love turned e'en water into wine.
O poesy is on the wane;
I cannot find her face again.

The sun those mornings used to find,
When clouds were other-country-mountains,
And heaven looked upon the mind
With groves and rocks and mottled fountains.
These heavens are gone, the mountains grey
Turned mist; the sun a homeless ranger
Pursuing on a naked way
Unnoticed like a very stranger.
O poesy is on its wane;
Nor love nor joy is mine again.

Love's sun went down without a frown;
For very joy it used to grieve us.
I often think that west is gone.
Ah, cruel time to undeceive us.
The stream it is a naked stream
Where we on Sundays used to ramble,
The sky hangs o'er a broken dream,
The brambles dwindled to a bramble.
O poesy is on its wane;
I cannot find her haunts again.

Mere withered stalks and fading trees
And pastures spread with hills and rushes
Are all my fading vision sees.
Gone, gone is rapture's flooding gushes
When mushrooms they were fairy bowers,
Their marble pillars overswelling,
And danger paused to pluck the flowers
That in their swarthy rings were dwelling.
But poesy's spells are on the wane;
Nor joy nor fear is mine again.

Aye, poesy hath passed away
And fancy's visions undeceive us.
The night hath ta'en the place of day
And why should passing shadows grieve us?
I thought the flowers upon the hills
Were flowers from Adam's open gardens,
And I have had my Summer thrills
And I have had my heart's rewardings.
So poesy is on its wane;
I hardly know her face again.

And friendship it hath burned away
Just like a very ember cooling,
A make-believe on April day
That sent the simple heart a-fooling,
Mere jesting in an earnest way,
Deceiving on and still deceiving;
And hope is but a fancy play
And joy the art of true believing;
For poesy is on the wane.
O could I feel her faith again.

Song: Last Day

There is a day, a dreadful day,
Still following the past,
When sun and moon are past away
And mingle with the blast.
There is a vision in my eye,
A vacuum o'er my mind,
Sometimes as on the sea I lie
'Mid roaring waves and wind,

When valleys rise to mountain waves
And mountains sink to seas,
When towns and cities, temples, graves

All vanish like a breeze.
The skies that was are past and o'er;
That almanac of days,
Year chronicles are kept no more;
Oblivion's ruin pays,

Pays in destruction shades and hell;
Sin goes in darkness down,
And there in sulphur's shadows dwell.
Worth wins and wears the crown.
The very shore, if shore I see,
All shrivelled to a scroll;
The Heavens rend away from me
And thunder's sulphurs roll.

Black as the deadly thunder cloud
The stars shall turn to dun
And heaven by that darkness bowed
Shall make day's light be done.
When stars and skies shall all decay
And earth no more shall be,
When heaven itself shall pass away
Then thou'lt remember me.

The Fallen Elm

Old Elm that murmured in our chimney top
The sweetest anthem Autumn ever made
And into mellow whispering calms would drop
When showers fell on thy many-coloured shade,
And when dark tempests mimic thunder made
While darkness came as it would strangle light
With the black tempest of a Winter night
That rocked thee like a cradle to thy root,
How did I love to hear the winds upbraid
Thy strength without, while all within was mute;

It seasoned comfort to our hearts' desire.
We felt thy kind protection like a friend
And pitched our chairs up closer to the fire,
Enjoying comforts that was never penned.
Old favourite tree, thou'st seen time's changes lour
Though change till now did never injure thee,
For time beheld thee as her sacred dower
And nature claimed thee her domestic tree.
Storms came and shook thee many a weary hour
Yet steadfast to thy home thy roots hath been.
Summers of thirst parched round thy homely bower
Till earth grew iron; still thy leaves was green.
The childern sought thee in thy Summer shade
And made their playhouse rings of sticks and stone;
The mavis sang and felt himself alone
While in thy leaves his early nest was made
And I did feel his happiness mine own,
Nought heeding that our friendship was betrayed.
Friend not inanimate, though stocks and stones
There are and many formed of flesh and bones,
Thou owned a language by which hearts are stirred
Deeper than by a feeling clothed in words;
And speakest now what's known of every tongue,
Language of pity and the force of wrong;
What cant assumes, what hypocrites may dare
Speaks home to truth and shows it what they are.
I see a picture that thy fate displays
And learn a lesson from thy destiny:
Self interest saw thee stand in freedom's ways
So thy old shadow must a tyrant be.
Thou'st heard the knave, abusing those in power,
Bawl freedom loud and then oppress the free.
Thou'st sheltered hypocrites in many a shower
That when in power would never shelter thee.
Thou'st heard the knave supply his canting powers
With wrong's illusions when he wanted friends,
That bawled for shelter when he lived in showers
And when clouds vanished made thy shade amends;
With axe at root he felled thee to the ground
And barked of freedom – O I hate that sound;

Time hears its visions speak, and age sublime
Had made thee a disciple unto time.
– It grows the cant terms of enslaving tools
To wrong another by the name of right;
It grows the licence of o'erbearing fools
To cheat plain honesty by force of might.
Thus came enclosure – ruin was its guide
But freedom's clapping hands enjoyed the sight,
Though comfort's cottage soon was thrust aside
And workhouse prisons raised upon the site.
E'en nature's dwellings far away from men,
The common heath, became the spoilers' prey;
The rabbit had not where to make his den
And labour's only cow was drove away.
No matter – wrong was right and right was wrong
And freedom's bawl was sanction to the song.
Such was thy ruin, music-making Elm.
The rights of freedom was to injure thine.
As thou wert served, so would they overwhelm
In freedom's name the little that is mine.
And there are knaves that brawl for better laws
And cant of tyranny in stronger powers,
Who glut their vile unsatiated maws
And freedom's birthright from the weak devours.

The Lament of Swordy Well

Petitioners are full of prayers
To fall in pity's way,
But if her hand the gift forbears
They'll sooner swear than pray.
They're not the worst to want, who lurch
On plenty with complaints;
No more than those who go to church
Are e'er the better saints.

I hold no hat to beg a mite
Nor pick it up when thrown
Nor limping leg I hold in sight
But pray to keep my own;
Where profit gets his clutches in
There's little he will leave;
Gain stooping for a single pin
Will stick it on his sleeve.

For passers-by I never pin
No troubles to my breast
Nor carry round some names to win
More money from the rest;
I'm Swordy Well, a piece of land
That's fell upon the town,
Who worked me till I couldn't stand
And crush me now I'm down.

In parish bonds I well may wail,
Reduced to every shift;
Pity may grieve at trouble's tale
But cunning shares the gift.
Harvests with plenty on his brow
Leaves losses' taunts with me,
Yet gain comes yearly with the plough
And will not let me be.

Alas dependence, thou'rt a brute
Want only understands;
His feelings wither branch and root
That falls in parish hands.
The muck that clouts the ploughman's shoe,
The moss that hides the stone,
Now I'm become the parish due
Is more than I can own.

Though I'm no man, yet any wrong
Some sort of right may seek
And I am glad if e'en a song
Gives me the room to speak.

I've got among such grubbling gear
And such a hungry pack,
If I brought harvests twice a year
They'd bring me nothing back.

When war their tyrant prices got,
I trembled with alarms;
They fell, and saved my little spot
Or towns had turned to farms.
Let profit keep an humble place
That gentry may be known;
Let pedigrees their honours trace
And toil enjoy its own.

The silver springs, grown naked dykes,
Scarce own a bunch of rushes;
When grain got high the tasteless tykes
Grubbed up trees, banks and bushes,
And me, they turned me inside out
For sand and grit and stones
And turned my old green hills about
And picked my very bones.

These things that claim my own as theirs
Were born but yesterday,
But ere I fell to town affairs
I were as proud as they;
I kept my horses, cows and sheep
And built the town below
Ere they had cat or dog to keep;
And then to use me so.

Parish allowance, gaunt and dread,
Had it the earth to keep,
Would even pine the bees to dead
To save an extra keep.
Pride's workhouse is a place that yields
From poverty its gains,
And mine's a workhouse for the fields,
A starving the remains.

The bees fly round in feeble rings
And find no blossom by,
Then thrum their almost-weary wings
Upon the moss and die.
Rabbits that find my hills turned o'er
Forsake my poor abode;
They dread a workhouse like the poor
And nibble on the road.

If with a clover bottle now
Spring dares to lift her head,
The next day brings the hasty plough
And makes me misery's bed.
The butterflies may whirr and come,
I cannot keep 'em now,
Nor can they bear my parish home
That withers on my brow.

No, now not e'en a stone can lie;
I'm just whate'er they like.
My hedges like the Winter fly
And leave me but the dyke.
My gates are thrown from off the hooks,
The parish thoroughfare.
Lord, he that's in the parish books
Has little wealth to spare.

I couldn't keep a dust of grit
Nor scarce a grain of sand
But bags and carts claimed every bit
And now they've got the land.
I used to bring the Summer's life
To many a butterfly
But in oppression's iron strife
Dead tussocks bow and sigh.

I've scarce a nook to call my own
For things that creep or fly.
The beetle hiding 'neath a stone
Does well to hurry by.

Stock eats my struggles every day
As bare as any road.
He's sure to be in something's way
If e'er he stirs abroad.

I am no man to whine and beg
But fond of freedom still
I hing no lies on pity's peg
To bring a grist to mill.
On pity's back I needn't jump;
My looks speak loud alone.
My only tree they've left a stump
And nought remains my own.

My mossy hills gain's greedy hand
And more than greedy mind
Levels into a russet land,
Nor leaves a bent behind.
In Summers gone I bloomed in pride;
Folks came for miles to prize
My flowers that bloomed nowhere beside
And scarce believed their eyes.

Yet worried with a greedy pack
They rend and delve and tear
The very grass from off my back;
I've scarce a rag to wear.
Gain takes my freedom all away
Since its dull suit I wore
And yet scorn vows I never pay
And hurts me more and more.

And should the price of grain get high
(Lord help and keep it low)
I shan't possess a single fly
Or get a weed to grow;
I shan't possess a yard of ground
To bid a mouse to thrive
For gain has put me in a pound;
I scarce can keep alive.

I own I'm poor like many more
But then the poor mun live
And many came for miles before
For what I had to give;
But since I fell upon the town
They pass me with a sigh;
I've scarce the room to say 'Sit down'
And so they wander by.

Though now I seem so full of clack,
Yet when you're riding by
The very birds upon my back
Are not more fain to fly.
I feel so lorn in this disgrace,
God send the grain to fall.
I am the oldest in the place
And the worst-served of all.

Lord bless ye, I was kind to all
And poverty in me
Could always find a humble stall,
A rest and lodging free.
Poor bodies with an hungry ass
I welcomed many a day
And gave him tether-room and grass
And never said him nay.

There was a time my bit of ground
Made freemen of the slave.
The ass no pindar'd dare to pound
When I his supper gave.
The gipsies' camp was not afraid;
I made his dwelling free,
Till vile enclosure came and made
A parish slave of me.

The gipsies further on sojourn;
No parish bounds they like.
No sticks I own and would earth burn
I shouldn't own a dyke.

I am no friend to lawless work
Nor would a rebel be,
And why I call a christian turk
Is they are turks to me.

And if I could but find a friend
With no deceit to sham,
Who'd send me some few sheep to tend
And leave me as I am,
To keep my hills from cart and plough
And strife of mongrel men
And, as Spring found me, find me now,
I should look up again.

And save his Lordship's woods that past
The day of danger dwell,
Of all the fields I am the last
That my own face can tell.
Yet, what with stone pits, delving holes
And strife to buy and sell,
My name will quickly be the whole
That's left of Swordy Well.

The Moors

Far spread the moory ground a level scene,
Bespread with rush and one eternal green,
That never felt the rage of blundering plough
Though centuries wreathed Spring's blossoms on its brow,
Still meeting plains that stretched them far away
In unchecked shadows of green, brown and grey.
Unbounded freedom ruled the wandering scene
Nor fence of ownership crept in between
To hide the prospect of the following eye;
Its only bondage was the circling sky.
One mighty flat undwarfed by bush and tree

Spread its faint shadow of immensity
And lost itself, which seemed to eke its bounds,
In the blue mist the horizon's edge surrounds.
Now this sweet vision of my boyish hours,
Free as Spring clouds and wild as Summer flowers,
Is faded all – a hope that blossomed free
And hath been once no more shall ever be.
Enclosure came and trampled on the grave
Of labour's rights and left the poor a slave;
And memory's pride, ere want to wealth did bow,
Is both the shadow and the substance now.
The sheep and cows were free to range as then
Where change might prompt, nor felt the bonds of men.
Cows went and came with evening, morn and night
To the wild pasture as their common right
And sheep, unfolded with the rising sun,
Heard the swains shout and felt their freedom won,
Tracked the red fallow field and heath and plain,
Then met the brook and drank and roamed again –
The brook that dribbled on as clear as glass
Beneath the roots they hid among the grass –
While the glad shepherd traced their tracks along,
Free as the lark and happy as her song.
But now all's fled and flats of many a dye
That seemed to lengthen with the following eye,
Moors losing from the sight, far, smooth and blea,
Where swopt the plover in its pleasure free,
Are vanished now with commons wild and gay
As poets' visions of life's early day.
Mulberry bushes where the boy would run
To fill his hands with fruit are grubbed and done,
And hedgerow briars – flower-lovers overjoyed
Came and got flower pots – these are all destroyed,
And sky-bound moors in mangled garbs are left
Like mighty giants of their limbs bereft.
Fence now meets fence in owners' little bounds
Of field and meadow, large as garden grounds,
In little parcels little minds to please
With men and flocks imprisoned, ill at ease.
Each little path that led its pleasant way

As sweet as morning leading night astray,
Where little flowers bloomed round, a varied host,
That travel felt delighted to be lost
Nor grudged the steps that he had ta'en as vain
When right roads traced his journey's end again;
Nay on a broken tree he'd sit awhile
To see the moors and fields and meadows smile,
Sometimes with cowslips smothered – then all white
With daisies – then the Summer's splendid sight
Of corn fields crimson o'er the 'headache' bloomed
Like splendid armies for the battle plumed;
He gazed upon them with wild fancy's eye
As fallen landscapes from an evening sky;
These paths are stopped – the rude philistine's thrall
Is laid upon them and destroyed them all.
Each little tyrant with his little sign
Shows, where man claims, earth glows no more divine.
On paths to freedom and to childhood dear
A board sticks up to notice 'no road here'
And on the tree with ivy overhung
The hated sign by vulgar taste is hung
As though the very birds should learn to know
When they go there they must no further go.
Thus, with the poor, scared freedom bade good bye
And much they feel it in the smothered sigh,
And birds and trees and flowers without a name
All sighed when lawless law's enclosure came;
And dreams of plunder in such rebel schemes
Have found too truly that they were but dreams.

John Clare, Poet

'I Am'

I am – yet what I am, none cares or knows;
   My friends forsake me like a memory lost: –
I am the self-consumer of my woes; –
   They rise and vanish in oblivion's host,
Like shadows in love's frenzied stifled throes: –
And yet I am, and live – like vapours tossed

Into the nothingness of scorn and noise, –
   Into the living sea of waking dreams,
Where there is neither sense of life or joys,
   But the vast shipwreck of my life's esteems;
Even the dearest, that I love the best
Are strange – nay, rather stranger than the rest.

I long for scenes, where man hath never trod,
   A place where woman never smiled or wept,
There to abide with my Creator, God;
   And sleep as I in childhood, sweetly slept,
Untroubling, and untroubled where I lie,
The grass below – above the vaulted sky.

A Vision

I lost the love, of heaven above;
I spurned the lust, of earth below;
I felt the sweets of fancied love, –
And hell itself my only foe.

I lost earth's joys, but felt the glow,
Of heaven's flame abound in me:
'Till loveliness, and I did grow,
The bard of immortality.

I loved, but woman fell away;
I hid me, from her faded fame:
I snatched the sun's eternal ray, –
And wrote 'till earth was but a name.

In every language upon earth,
On every shore, o'er every sea;
I gave my name immortal birth,
And kept my spirit with the free.

To John Clare

Well, honest John, how fare you now at home?
The Spring is come and birds are building nests,
The old cock robin to the sty is come
With olive feathers and its ruddy breast,
And the old cock with wattles and red comb
Struts with the hens and seems to like some best,
Then crows and looks about for little crumbs
Swept out by little folks an hour ago.
The pigs sleep in the sty; the bookman comes,
The little boys lets home-close-nesting go
And pockets tops and taws where daisies bloom
To look at the new number just laid down
With lots of pictures and good stories too
And Jack the Giant-killer's high renown.

Song: 'A seaboy on the giddy mast'

A seaboy on the giddy mast
Sees nought but ocean waves
And hears the wild inconstant blast
Where loud the tempest raves.

My life is like the ocean wave
And like the inconstant sea:
In every hope appears a grave
And leaves no hope for me.

My life is like the ocean's lot:
Bright gleams the morning gave
But storms o'erwhelmed the sunny spot
Deep in the ocean wave.

My life hath been the ocean storm,
A black and troubled sea.
When shall I find my life a calm,
A port and harbour free?

The Peasant Poet

He loved the brook's soft sound,
The swallow swimming by;
He loved the daisy-covered ground,
The cloud-bedappled sky.
To him the dismal storm appeared
The very voice of God,
And where the Evening rock was reared
Stood Moses with his rod;
And every thing his eyes surveyed –
The insects i' the brake –

Were creatures God almighty made;
He loved them for his sake.
A silent man in life's affairs,
A thinker from a Boy,
A Peasant in his daily cares –
The Poet in his joy.

Sighing for Retirement

O take me from the busy crowd,
    I cannot bear the noise!
For Nature's voice is never loud;
    I seek for quiet joys.

The book I love is everywhere,
    And not in idle words;
The book I love is known to all,
    And better lore affords.

The book I love is everywhere,
    And every place the same;
God bade me make my dwelling there,
    And look for better fame.

I never feared the critic's pen,
    To live by my renown;
I found the poems in the fields,
    And only wrote them down.

And quiet Epping pleases well,
    Where Nature's love delays;
I joy to see the quiet place,
    And wait for better days.

I love to seek the brakes and fern,
    And rabbits up and down;

And then the pleasant Autumn comes,
    And turns them all to brown.

To common eyes they only seem
    A desert waste and drear;
To taste and love they always shine,
    A garden through the year.

Lord keep my love for quiet joys,
    Oh, keep me to thy will!
I know Thy works, and always find
    Thy mercies kinder still!

Song's Eternity

What is song's eternity?
Come and see.
Can it noise and bustle be?
Come and see.
Praises sung or praises said
Can it be?
Wait awhile and these are dead
(Sigh, sigh);
Be they high or lowly bred
They die.

What is song's eternity?
Come and see.
Melodies of earth and sky,
Here they be:
Songs once sung to Adam's ears
Can it be?
– Ballads of six thousand years
Thrive, thrive,
Songs awakened with the spheres
Alive.

Mighty songs that miss decay,
What are they?
Crowds and cities pass away
Like a day.
Books are writ and books are read;
What are they?
Years will lay them with the dead
(Sigh, sigh);
Trifles unto nothing wed,
They die.

Dreamers, list the honey bee;
Mark the tree
Where the blue cap (tootle tee)
Sings a glee
Sung to Adam and to Eve;
Here they be.
When floods covered every bough,
Noah's ark
Heard that ballad singing now.
Hark, hark.

Tootle tootle tootle tee;
Can it be
Pride and fame must shadows be?
Come and see
Every season own her own
Bird and bee
Sing creation's music on;
Nature's glee
Is in every mood and tone
Eternity.

The eternity of song
Liveth here.
Nature's universal tongue
Singeth here
Songs I've heard and felt and seen
Everywhere;

Songs like the grass are evergreen;
The giver
Said live and be, and they have been
For ever.

Glinton Spire

Glinton, thy taper spire predominates
Over the level landscape – and the mind
Musing – the pleasing picture contemplates
Like elegance of beauty much refined
By taste – that almost deifies and elevates,
One's admiration making common things
Around it glow with beauties not their own.
Thus, all around, the earth superior springs;
Those straggling trees, though lonely, seem not lone
But in thy presence wear superior power
And e'en each mossed and melancholy stone,
Gleaning cold memories round oblivion's bower
Seem types of fair eternity – and hire
A lease from fame by thy enchanting spire.

The Eternity of Nature

Leaves from eternity are simple things
To the world's gaze, whereto a spirit clings,
Sublime and lasting. Trampled underfoot
The daisy lives and strikes its little root
Into the lap of time. Centuries may come
And pass away into the silent tomb

And still the child, hid in the womb of time,
Shall smile and pluck them when this simple rhyme
Shall be forgotten like a churchyard stone
Or lingering lie unnoticed and alone,
When eighteen hundred years, our common date,
Grows many thousands in their marching state.
Aye, still the child with pleasure in his eye
Shall cry 'The daisy' – a familiar cry –
And run to pluck it, in the self same state
As when time found it in his infant date,
And like a child himself when all was new
Wonder might smile and make him notice too.
Its little golden bosom frilled with snow
Might win e'en Eve to stoop adown and show
Her partner Adam in the silky grass
This little gem that smiled where pleasure was,
And loving Eve from Eden followed ill
And bloomed with sorrow and lives smiling still
As once in Eden under Heaven's breath,
So now on blighted earth and on the lap of death
It smiles for ever. Cowslips' golden blooms
That in the closen and the meadow comes
Shall come when kings and empires fade and die
And in the meadows as time's partners lie,
As fresh two thousand years to come as now
With those five crimson spots upon its brow.
And little brooks that hum a simple lay
In green unnoticed spots from praise away
Shall sing when poets, in time's darkness hid,
Shall lie like memory in a pyramid,
Forgetting yet not all forgot, though lost
Like a thread's end, in ravelled windings crossed.
And the small humble bee shall hum as long
As nightingales, for time protects the song;
And nature is their soul to whom all clings
Of fair or beautiful in lasting things.
The little robin in the quiet glen,
Hidden from fame and all the sons of men,

Sings unto time a pastoral and gives
A music that lives on and ever lives.
Both Spring and Autumn years rich bloom and fade
Longer than songs that poets ever made,
And think ye these, time's play things, pass proud skill;
Time loves them like a child and ever will.
And so I worship them in bushy spots
And sing with them when all else notice not
And feel the music of their mirth agree
With that sooth quiet that bestirreth me.
And if I touch aright that quiet tone,
That soothing truth that shadows forth their own,
Then many a year shall grow in after days
And still find hearts to love my quiet lays,
Yet cheering mirth with thoughts sung, not for fame,
But for the joy that with their utterance came,
That inward breath of rapture urged not loud
– Birds singing lone fly silent past a crowd.
So in these pastoral spots which childish time
Makes dear to me I wander out and rhyme
What time the dewy morning's infancy
Hangs on each blade of grass and every tree
And sprents the red thighs of the bumble bee
Who 'gins betimes unwearied minstrelsy,
Who breakfasts, dines and most divinely sups
With every flower save golden buttercups;
On their proud bosoms he will never go
But passes by with scarcely 'How do ye do'.
So in their showy gaudy shining cells
May be the Summer's honey never dwells
– Her ways are mysteries all, yet endless youth
Lives in them all unchangeable as truth.
With the odd number five strange nature's laws
Plays many freaks nor once mistakes the cause,
And in the cowslip peeps this very day
Five spots appear which time ne'er wears away,
Nor once mistakes the counting – look within
Each peep and five nor more nor less is seen.
And trailing bindweed with its pinky cup,

Five lines of paler hue goes streaking up;
And birds a-many keep the rule alive
And lay five eggs nor more nor less than five.
And flowers how many own that mystic power,
With five leaves ever making up the flower.
The five-leaved grass trailing its golden cups
Of flowers – five leaves make all for which I stoop.
And briony in the hedge, that now adorns
The tree to which it clings and now the thorns
Own five star-pointed leaves of dingy white;
Count which I will, all make the number right.
And spreading goosegrass trailing all abroad
In leaves of silver green about the road,
Five leaves make every blossom all along;
I stoop for many; none are counted wrong.
'Tis nature's wonder and her maker's will
Who bade earth be, and order owns him still
As that superior power who keeps the key
Of wisdom, power and might through all eternity.

Shadows of Taste

Taste with as many hues doth hearts engage
As leaves and flowers do upon nature's page.
Not mind alone the instinctive mood declares,
But birds and flowers and insects are its heirs.
Taste is their joyous heritage and they
All choose for joy in a peculiar way.
Birds own it in the various spots they choose:
Some live content in low grass gemmed with dews;
The yellowhammer like a tasteful guest
'Neath picturesque green molehills makes a nest
Where oft the shepherd with unlearned ken
Finds strange eggs scribbled as with ink and pen.

He looks with wonder on the learned marks
And calls them in his memory 'writing larks'.
Birds bolder-winged on bushes love to be
While some choose cradles on the highest tree;
There rocked by winds they feel no moods of fear
But joy their birthright lives for ever near;
And the bold eagle which man's fear enshrouds
Would, could he lodge it, house upon the clouds,
While little wrens mistrusting none that come
In each low hovel meet a sheltered home.

   Flowers in the wisdom of creative choice
Seem blest with feeling and a silent voice.
Some on the barren roads delight to bloom
And others haunt the melancholy tomb,
Where death, the blight of all, finds Summer's hours
Too kind to miss him with her host of flowers.
Some flourish in the sun and some the shade
Who almost in his morning smiles would fade;
These in leaf-darkened woods right timid stray
And in its green night smile their lives away.
Others in water live and scarcely seem
To peep their little flowers above the stream,
While water lilies in their glories come
And spread green isles of beauty round their home.
All share the Summer's glory and its good
And taste of joy in each peculiar mood.

   Insects of varied taste in rapture share
The heyday luxuries which she comes to heir.
In wild disorder various routs they run,
In water, earth, still shade and busy sun,
And in the crowds of green earth's busy claims
They e'en grow nameless mid their many names;
And man, that noble insect, restless man,
Whose thoughts scale heaven in its mighty span,
Pours forth his living soul in many a shade
And taste runs riot in her every grade;
While the low herd, mere savages subdued,
With nought of feeling or of taste imbued,
Pass over sweetest scenes a careless eye

As blank as midnight in its deepest dye.
From these and different far in rich degrees,
Minds spring as various as the leaves of trees,
To follow taste and all her sweets explore
And Edens make where deserts spread before.
    In poesy's spells some all their raptures find
And revel in the melodies of mind;
There nature o'er the soul her beauty flings
In all the sweets and essences of things.
A face of beauty in a city crowd –
Met, passed and vanished like a Summer cloud –
In poesy's vision more refined and fair
Taste reads o'erjoyed and greets her image there.
Dashes of sunshine and a page of May
Live there a whole life long one Summer's day.
A blossom in its witchery of bloom,
There gathered, dwells in beauty and perfume.
The singing bird, the brook that laughs along
There ceaseless sing and never thirsts for song.
A pleasing image to its page conferred
In living character and breathing word
Becomes a landscape heard and felt and seen,
Sunshine and shade one harmonizing green,
Where meads and brooks and forests basking lie,
Lasting as truth and the eternal sky.
Thus truth to nature as the true sublime
Stands a mount Atlas overpeering time.
    Styles may with fashions vary – tawdry, chaste
Have had their votaries which each fancied taste;
From Donne's old homely gold whose broken feet
Jostles the reader's patience from its seat,
To Pope's smooth rhymes that regularly play
In music's stated periods all the way,
That starts and closes, starts again and times
Its tuning gamut true as minster chimes.
From these old fashions stranger metres flow,
Half prose, half verse, that stagger as they go;
One line starts smooth and then, for room perplexed,
Elbows along and knocks against the next

And half its neighbour, where a pause marks time.
There the clause ends; what follows is for rhyme.
Yet truth to nature will in all remain,
As grass in Winter glorifies the plain,
And over fashion's foils rise proud and high
As light's bright fountain in a cloudy sky.
   The man of science in discovery's moods
Roams o'er the furze-clad heath, leaf-buried woods,
And by the simple brook in rapture finds
Treasures that wake the laugh of vulgar hinds,
Who see no further in his dark employs
Than village childern seeking after toys.
Their clownish hearts and ever heedless eyes
Find nought in nature they as wealth can prize.
With them self interest and the thoughts of gain
Are nature's beauties; all beside are vain.
But he, the man of science and of taste,
Sees wealth far richer in the worthless waste,
Where bits of lichen and a sprig of moss
Will all the raptures of his mind engross,
And bright-winged insects on the flowers of May
Shine pearls too wealthy to be cast away.
His joys run riot mid each juicy blade
Of grass where insects revel in the shade;
And minds of different moods will oft condemn
His taste as cruel – such the deeds to them –
While he unconscious gibbets butterflies
And strangles beetles all to make us wise.
Taste's rainbow visions own unnumbered hues
And every shade its sense of taste pursues.
The heedless mind may laugh, the clown may stare;
They own no soul to look for pleasure there;
Their grosser feelings in a coarser dress
Mock at the wisdom which they can't possess.
   Some in recordless rapture love to breathe
Nature's wild Eden, wood and field and heath;
In common blades of grass his thoughts will raise
A world of beauty to admire and praise,
Until his heart o'erflows with swarms of thought

To that great being who raised life from nought.
The common weed adds graces to his mind
And gleams in beauties few beside may find.
Associations sweet each object breeds
And fine ideas upon fancy feeds.
He loves not flowers because they shed perfumes,
Or butterflies alone for painted plumes,
Or birds for singing, although sweet it be,
But he doth love the wild and meadow lea;
There hath the flower its dwelling place and there
The butterfly goes dancing through the air.
He loves each desolate neglected spot
That seems in labour's hurry left forgot:
The warped and punished trunk of stunted oak,
Freed from its bonds but by the thunder stroke,
As crampt by straggling ribs of ivy sere;
There the glad bird makes home for half the year.
But, take these several beings from their homes,
Each beauteous thing a withered thought becomes;
Association fades and like a dream
They are but shadows of the things they seem.
Torn from their homes and happiness they stand
The poor dull captives of a foreign land.
    Some spruce and delicate ideas feed;
With them disorder is an ugly weed,
And wood and heath a wilderness of thorns,
Which gardeners' shears nor fashions nor adorns.
No spots give pleasure so forlorn and bare
But gravel walks would work rich wonders there.
With such, wild nature's beauty's run to waste
And art's strong impulse mars the truth of taste.
Such are the various moods that taste displays,
Surrounding wisdom in concentrating rays,
Where threads of light from one bright focus run
As day's proud halo circles round the sun.

To be Placed at the Back of his Portrait

Bard of the mossy cot,
Known through all ages,
Leaving no line to blot
All through thy pages.
Bard of the fallow field
And the green meadow
Where the sweet birds build,
Nature thy widow.

Bard of the wild flowers,
Rain-washed and wind-shaken;
Dear to thee was mild showers
And heaths o' green bracken.
The song o' the wild bird
Than nothing seemed dearer:
The low o' the mild herd
And sheep bleating nearer.

Bard o' the sheep pen,
The stack yard and stable,
The hovel in bracken glen
Where a stone makes a table.
There the white daisy blooms
With a tear in his eye;
There Jenny Wren comes
When Winter is by;

Comes there and builds anew
His pudding-bag nest
Hidden from rain and dew
The milking cows' guest.
Bard o' the mossy shed,
Live on for ages;
Daisies bloom by thy bed
And live in thy pages.

Memory

I would not that my being all should die
And pass away with every common lot;
I would not that my humble dust should lie
In quite a strange and unfrequented spot,
By all unheeded and by all forgot,
With nothing save the heedless winds to sigh
And nothing but the dewy morn to weep
About my grave, far hid from the world's eye.
I feign would have some friend to wander nigh
And find a path to where my ashes sleep:
Not the cold heart that merely passes by
To read who lieth there, but such that keep
Past memories warm with deeds of other years
And pay to friendship some few friendly tears.

Notes

This selection from John Clare's works is meant to be introductory. The texts for the poems have been based where possible on the authoritative standard texts edited by Eric Robinson and his colleagues, or where these are not yet available, on *The Oxford Authors John Clare*, edited by Eric Robinson and David Powell, or on Robinson and Powell's *Northborough Sonnets* or my own edition of *The Midsummer Cushion*. It is my hope that readers will be encouraged to read further in Clare, and anyone who is so encouraged will wish to consult these editions and see what it is like to read Clare with his own spelling and his own punctuation (or lack of it). The best single edition to pursue further reading of Clare is *The Oxford Authors John Clare*, and there is also Geoffrey Summerfield's Penguin Poetry Library edition (1990). All the poetry will be found in the Clarendon Press series, which has now reached the sixth of its soon-to-be-completed nine volumes. I list the editions below and indicate in the notes where my texts derive from. I have introduced a sparing amount of punctuation (the editors who have spent the best part of a lifetime getting rid of editorial interposing between Clare and his reader will I hope forgive the experiment) and have normalised the spelling, while retaining spellings which the rhyme or rhythm demanded, and dialect words or formulations, which are a necessary feature of Clare's identity. I have added a glossary to help with the dialect terms.

The six volumes of the Complete Poems published so far are:

The Early Poems of John Clare 1804–1822, ed. Eric Robinson, David Powell and Margaret Grainger, 2 vols, Clarendon Press, Oxford, 1989 (abbreviated as *EP*).

John Clare Poems of the Middle Period 1822–1837, ed. Robinson, Powell and P. M. S. Dawson, 2 vols, Clarendon Press, Oxford, 1996 (abbreviated as *MP*).

The Later Poems of John Clare 1837–1864, ed. Robinson, Powell and Grainger, 2 vols, Clarendon Press, Oxford, 1984 (abbreviated as *LP*).

I have also selected from:

The Midsummer Cushion, ed. Anne Tibble and R. K. R. Thornton, MidNAG and Carcanet, Ashington and Manchester, 1978 and 1990 (abbreviated as *MC*).

The Oxford Authors John Clare, ed. Robinson and Powell, Oxford University Press, 1984 (abbreviated as *OA*).

The Northborough Sonnets, ed. Robinson, Powell and Dawson, MidNAG and Carcanet, Ashington and Manchester, 1995 (abbreviated as *NS*).

Clare's other writings can be found in:

The Natural History Prose Writings of John Clare, ed. Margaret Grainger, Clarendon Press, Oxford, 1983.

The Letters of John Clare, ed. Mark Storey, Clarendon Press, Oxford, 1985.

John Clare, Cottage Tales, ed. Robinson, Powell and Dawson, MidNAG and Carcanet, Ashington and Manchester, 1993.

John Clare By Himself, ed. Robinson and Powell, MidNAG and Carcanet, Ashington and Manchester, 1996 (abbreviated as JCBH).

The following books will provide a good start in Clare criticism:

The Idea of Landscape and the Sense of Place, by John Barrell, Cambridge University Press, 1972.

The Poetry of John Clare: A Critical Introduction, by Mark Storey, Macmillan, London, 1974.

John Clare and the Folk Tradition, by George Deacon, Sinclair Browne, London, 1983 (abbreviated as *Deacon*).

'*A real world & doubting mind*', by Tim Chilcott, Hull University Press, 1985.

John Clare and the Bounds of Circumstance, by Johanne Clare, McGill-Queen's University Press, Kingston and Montreal, 1987.

John Clare in Context, ed. Hugh Haughton, Adam Phillips and Geoffrey Summerfield, Cambridge University Press, 1994.

Anyone wishing to further their interest in Clare should contact the John Clare Society through Peter Moyse, The Stables, Helpston, PE6 7DU, or James McKusick, English Department, University of Maryland, Baltimore, MD, 21228, USA.

A Country Village Year

***December* from '*The Shepherd's Calendar*': *Christmas*:** *MP*, I, pp.156–162. See Clare's note on customs and village games in *Deacon*, pp.283ff and *passim*.

Sonnet: 'The barn door is open': *NS*, p. 35.

The Wheat Ripening: *MC*, p. 438.

The Beans in Blossom: *MC*, p. 401.

Sonnet: 'The landscape laughs in Spring': *MP*, II, p. 108.

Sonnet: 'I dreaded walking where there was no path': *NS*, p. 83.

Sonnet: 'The passing traveller': *NS*, p. 98.

Sport in the Meadows: *MC*, pp. 198–9. I have left Clare's older forms, 'maken', 'abouten', 'renten', 'folken', 'helpen' as necessary for the metre.

Emmonsales Heath: *MC*, pp. 160–2.

Summer Tints: *EP*, II, p. 374.

The Summer Shower: *MC*, p. 183.

Summer Moods: *MC*, p. 383.

Sonnet: 'The maiden ran away': *NS*, p. 85.

Song: 'She tied up her few things': *LP*, p. 898.

The Foddering Boy: *EP*, II, p. 585.

The Gipsy Camp: *LP*, p. 29.

Winter Fields: *MC*, p. 485.

The Cottager: *MC*, pp. 177–9. l.19 St Thomas-tide is 21 December, the shortest day. l.63 Gessner's *Death of Abel* was translated in about 1814 and often selected from as a chapbook. It was preferred by the boy Clare to *Paradise Lost*. See *JCBH*, pp.16, 198 and 288–9. l.65 The 1812 edition of Thomas Tusser's *Five Hundred Points of Good Husbandry* was in Clare's library. l.81 Admiral Rodney, second only to Nelson in naval renown, defeated the French fleet under the Comte de Grasse on 12 April 1782 off Dominica, an action in which Lord Robert Manners, second son of the Marquis of Granby, was fatally wounded.

The Crow Sat on the Willow: *LP*, p. 837.

from *'The Parish'*: *EP*, II, pp. 698–709.

St Martin's Eve: *MC*, pp. 112–17. The feast of St Martin is the 11 November. In his letter to *The Every-day Book*, Clare describes village games and customs, and assigns the putting of a red onion beneath the pillow to dream of a future husband to St Thomas's eve; see *Deacon*, pp. 283ff. See also David Blamires's 'Chapbooks, Fairytales and Children's Books in the Writings of John Clare' in *The John Clare Society Journal*, Number 15, 1996, for the tales of Bluebeard and Tib.

Birds and Beasts

The Wren: *MC*, p. 391.

Sonnet: The Crow: *LP*, p. 498.

Sonnet: 'I love to hear the evening crows go by': *NS*, p. 67.
The Skylark: *MC*, p. 244.
Sonnet: 'Among the orchard weeds': *NS*, p. 86.
The Landrail: *MC*, pp. 267–8.
Sonnet: The Nightingale: *LP*, p. 372.
The Nightingale's Nest: *MC*, p. 201–3.
The Yellowhammer's Nest: *MC*, p. 239. Castalia is the spring on Mount
    Parnassus, sacred to the Muses. Clare uses the Spenserian spelling for
    both Castaly and Parnass.
The Pettichap's Nest: *MC*, pp. 240–1.
Sonnets: The Hedgehog: *NS*, pp. 29–30.
Sonnet: 'One day when all the woods were bare': *NS*, p. 84.
Sonnet: 'I found a ball of grass among the hay': *NS*, p. 54.
The Ants: *EP*, II, p. 56.
Little Trotty Wagtail: *LP*, p. 705.

Love

Song: 'The morning mist is changing blue': *LP*, p. 345.
First Love's Recollections: *MC*, pp. 302–3.
Ballad: 'I dreamt not what it was to woo': *MC*, p. 307.
Song: 'Say what is love': *LP*, p. 78.
Song: 'Love lives beyond': *LP*, pp. 406–7.
Ballad: 'The Spring returns, the pewit screams': *MC*, pp. 315–16.
An Invite to Eternity: *LP*, pp. 348–9.
Love and Memory: *MC*, pp. 189–91.

Loss and the Politics of Nature

Remembrances: *MC*, pp. 369–71. The names are all of places associated
    with the Helpston of Clare's boyhood. The boyish games are not totally
    clear. A bandy is a sort of hockey stick and clink is a single blow, so 'Clink
    and bandy' may be a game like 'knurr and spell' or 'buck and stick' where
    a piece of wood is tapped to make it rise and then struck as far as possible.
    'Chock' is a game of marbles, where the marbles are chocked or thrown
    into a hole. 'Taw' is a choice marble. 'Ducks' is a game played by trying to
    knock a fourth stone off a pile of three.
 The Flitting: *MC*, pp. 216–21.

Decay, a Ballad: *MC*, pp. 359–60.
Song: Last Day: *LP*, p. 175–6.
The Fallen Elm: *MC*, pp. 192–3.
The Lament of Swordy Well: *OA*, pp. 147–52. Swordy Well is an old stone quarry, usually known as Swaddy Well and famous for its wildlife.
The Moors: *OA*, pp. 167–9.

John Clare, Poet

'I Am': *LP*, pp. 396–7.
A Vision: *LP*, p. 297.
To John Clare: *LP*, pp. 1102–3. The John Clare addressed here is probably Clare's son, but the image is of his own youth.
Song: 'A seaboy on the giddy mast': *LP*, pp. 327–8.
The Peasant Poet: *LP*, p. 845.
Sighing for Retirement: *LP*, pp. 19–20.
Song's Eternity: *OA*, pp. 122–4.
Glinton Spire: *MC*, p. 428. The spire of Glinton church, visible from Helpston, marked the place where Clare met Mary Joyce.
The Eternity of Nature: *MC*, pp. 247–9.
Shadows of Taste: *MC*, pp. 130–3.
To be Placed at the Back of his Portrait: *LP*, pp. 696–7.
Memory: *MC*, p. 395.

Glossary

abouten, about

baulk, narrow strip of grass dividing two ploughed sections in open fields.

bent, grass stalk

besom ling, heather, used to make brooms

blackletter, gothic type common in books or broadsides until the 18th century

blea, exposed, bleak.

bottle, bottle-shaped blossom

brig, bridge

childern, standard plural for child

clack, talk, gossip

clout, clothe

crab, crab-apple

croodling, contracting the body from cold

cuckaball, an old game, or the ball it is played with, made of rags or flowers

cuckoo, lords and ladies, *Arum maculatum*

dead, death

dotterel, pollarded tree

elting, doughy, as of fresh-ploughed land

flitting, moving to a new house

frit, frightened

glib, smooth, slippery, voluble

grains, main branches

grubbling gear, scrounging (as in 'money-grubbing') crowd

gull, hollow out

'headache', poppy

hing, hang

hirkle, cower, crouch, shrink so as to keep warm

icle, icicle

knapweed, black knapweed, *Centaurea nigra*, or greater knapweed, *Centaurea scabiosa*

lady-smock, cuckoo-flower, *Cardamine pratensis*

lambtoe, birdsfoot trefoil, *Lotus corniculatus*

landrail, corncrake, *Crex crex*

lap, wrap

lated, belated

mavis, thrush

moise, moisten

mort, a great amount or number, crowd (usually in the plural)

mouldiwarp, mole

mun, must

old man's beard, traveller's joy, *Clematis vitalba*

peep, blossom

pettichap, chiffchaff, *Phylloscopus collybita*

pewit, lapwing, *Vanellus vanellus*

pindar, person employed to impound stray stock

pine, starve

pismire, ant

pleachy, bleached (?)

pooty, snail (shell)

pound, impound

prog, poke (to check the depth)

puddock, buzzard, *Buteo buteo*

pudge, little puddle

pudgy, muddy, full of puddles

ruckings, probably stooks of hay or corn

shepherd's purse, a common weed, *Capsella bursa-pastoris*

shoaf, sheaf

slive, sneak or creep slily

sluther, slide

snub, cut short

sosh, dip in flight, plunge suddenly

sprent, sprinkle

starnel, starling, *Sturnus vulgaris*

stoven, stump

stowk, stook

swee, swing

swop, swoop

taw, marble

water-blob, marsh marigold, *Caltha palustris*

wonder, wonderfully